D0871819

PLATO'S INTRODUCTION
TO THE QUESTION OF JUSTICE

Plato's Introduction

to the

Question

of

Justice

Devin Stauffer

STATE UNIVERSITY OF NEW YORK PRESS

Published by
State University of New York Press, Albany

Printed in the United States of America

For information, address State University of New York Press,
90 State Street, Suite 700, Albany, NY, 12207

Production by Cathleen Collins
Marketing by Fran Keneston

Library of Congress Cataloging in Publication Data

Stauffer, Devin, 1970–
    Plato's introduction to the question of justice / Devin Stauffer.
        p.   cm.
    Includes bibliographical references and index.
    ISBN 0–7914–4745–6 (alk. paper). — ISBN 0–7914–4746–4
    (pbk. : alk. paper)
    1. Plato—Contributions in concept of justice.   2. Justice (Philosophy)
    I. Title
    B398.J87.S73 2000
    172'.2'092—dc21   00–020254
                                                             CIP

10 9 8 7 6 5 4 3 2 1

Contents

Acknowledgments

I would like to thank the teachers and friends who helped me during the various stages of this work. In particular, I am grateful to David Bolotin, Timothy Burns, Eric Buzzetti, Susan Collins, Robert Faulkner, Michael Grenke, Lorna Knott, Ron Lee, and Susan Shell. The person from whom I received the most help, not only on this work but throughout my education in ancient political philosophy, is Christopher Bruell. I would also like to thank the readers for SUNY Press for their valuable suggestions. Finally, my greatest debts are to my fiancée and most ruthless editor, Dana Jalbert, and my parents, Robert and Trudy Stauffer.

Introduction

Plato's treatment of justice in the *Republic* is perhaps most famous for culminating in a number of strange and enchanting conclusions, as mysterious as they are paradoxical: that justice consists in the proper order of the soul, that there will be no end to the evils in the cities until philosophers rule, even that the truest or highest practice of justice is philosophy itself. The following work, however, is a study of the *Republic*'s humbler beginnings. For it is in these beginnings that Plato confronts most directly the ordinary opinions just men hold about justice; and it is here too that we find the battle lines first drawn up between Socrates and the attacks on justice that he devotes such energy to opposing in the rest of the *Republic*. Moreover, as each of these points in its way indicates, the *Republic*'s beginnings are of special importance to the movement or argument of the *Republic* as a whole. Humble as the *Republic*'s opening pages may be, they are also essential to the ascent to the later, more spectacular discussions of justice and philosophy: these later discussions, so paradoxical in that they depart so radically from the way justice is ordinarily understood, can only be justified by the examinations and challenges found in Book One and at the beginning of Book Two. The later parts of the *Republic* are arbitrary if they are not understood as dictated by (in the sense either of solutions to or elaborations of) the problems posed at the beginning.

Now, this very cursory explanation of the need to focus on the beginning of the *Republic* requires an answer to a more basic question: Why is it worth studying Plato's treatment of justice in the *Republic* at all? This question, essential to ask in any age, is especially pressing today. For despite Plato's continued fame, and even allowing for something of a resurgent interest in ancient thought, the general esteem in which Plato is held is at perhaps an all-time low. Let me begin my argument for the study of Plato, then, from the objections of some of his most vocal critics.

Stated simply and broadly, Plato's reputation suffers today because he is regarded as having inaugurated or at least led the most successful opening charge of the rationalist tradition in the West: Plato is widely seen as the classic example of a philosopher who overestimated the power of reason to discern the true, unchanging character of the world, and who believed, in particular, that reason could discover transcendent principles of justice or right through its direct access to nature. This is the indictment delivered, for example, by Richard Rorty, who argues that the "objectivist" or "foundationalist" tradition (in which he prominently includes Plato) is a vain attempt to do the impossible, to transcend one's particular historical community and arrive at universally valid principles of right. Against such hubris, Rorty urges us now to be more humble and to affirm that the only principles available to us have their source—their "foundation"—in nothing other than the particular circumstances and traditions of whatever community we happen to live in.[1] Or consider Michael Walzer, who speaks more pointedly of Plato's approach, which he contrasts with his own: "One way to begin the philosophic enterprise—perhaps the original way—is to walk out of the cave, leave the city, climb the mountain, fashion for oneself (what can never be fashioned for ordinary men and women) an objective and universal standpoint. . . . But I mean to stand in the cave, in the city, on the ground. Another way of doing philosophy is to interpret to one's fellow citizens the world of meanings that we share."[2]

---

1. For particulary clear statements of the opposition between "objectivism" and Rorty's version of pragmatism that stresses "solidarity," see Rorty's essays "Solidarity or Objectivity," "Non-reductive Physicalism," and "Postmodernist Bourgeois Liberalism," in *Objectivity, Relativism, and Truth* (New York: Cambridge University Press, 1991), pp. 21–34, 113–125, 197–202, as well as "The Contingency of a Liberal Community," and "Solidarity" in *Contingency, Irony, and Solidarity* (New York: Cambridge University Press, 1989), pp. 44–69, 189–198.

2. *Spheres of Justice* (New York: Basic Books, 1983), p. xiv. I am indebted to Steven Kautz, *Liberalism and Community* (Ithaca: Cornell University Press, 1995), p. 176, for alerting me to this source. See also Walzer, *Interpretation and Social Criticism* (Cambridge: Harvard University Press, 1987), pp. 3–32.

Now, as both Rorty and Walzer indicate and eagerly welcome, a new manner of "philosophy," understood by its proponents as a kind of anti-philosophy, is replacing what they argue is the original (and misguided) form philosophy took. This new form of philosophy can be described as the articulation of the moral understanding already present to us in the shared beliefs and accepted ways of our community or our historical culture; it is opposed, again, to the attempt to discover some transhistorical foundation (a theory of the self, e.g., or an account of human nature) from which the principles of justice can be derived. So prevalent has this new approach become that it bridges the oft-discussed divide between liberals and communitarians, making it at times difficult to draw a clear line between these two supposed poles of contemporary thought. We may be more likely, and it may be generally correct, to associate this new approach primarily with the communitarians, those who are leading the recent attempt to resuscitate the bonds of citizenship and community. But even in Rawls himself, the foremost of the liberals, we find a version of this approach in the central place he accords our "intuitive convictions" about justice, understood, especially in his more recent work, as the convictions of *us* as liberal democrats living *here* and living *now*.[3]

Indeed, it is particularly revealing of the currency and significance of this approach that Rawls has now been embraced by Rorty. In a well-known essay whose implications are nicely captured in its title, "The Priority of Democracy to Philosophy," Rorty enlists Rawls in his pragmatist opposition to "absolutism."[4] This essay is particularly instructive because in it Rorty and his Rawls stand in a certain respect beyond any simple framework separating "rationalist" liberals from their more "particularist" communitarian counterparts. Rorty presents his essay largely as an interpretation of Rawls, stressing what we might call the "communitarian basis" of Rawls's liberal thought:[5] against the view that Rawls is attempting to provide

---

3. See especially Rawls, "Justice as Fairness: Political not Metaphysical" *Philosophy and Public Affairs* 14 (1985): 223–251, and *Political Liberalism* (New York: Columbia University Press, 1993).

4. "The Priority of Democracy to Philosophy," found in *Objectivity, Relativism, and Truth*, pp. 175–196.

5. On the "communitarianism" of Rorty, see Kautz, *Liberalism and Community*, pp. 79–88.

a grounded and universal defense of liberal justice—a view to which Rorty admits he himself was first inclined in reading *A Theory of Justice*—Rorty argues that Rawls has corrected this misperception in his later work and has made it clear that he means to do no more than to "collect" and "organize" the convictions "we" share as twentieth-century heirs of Enlightenment liberalism.[6] Rorty's argument is also helpful as perhaps the starkest statement of the difference between this approach and the form he understands philosophy traditionally to have taken. Rorty insists, and he reads Rawls as insisting, that the best approach to "many standard topics of philosophical inquiry" is simply to "bracket [them] out." "For purposes of social theory," Rorty writes, "we can put aside such topics as an ahistorical human nature, the nature of selfhood, the motive of moral behavior, and the meaning of human life." He quotes Rawls's statement: " 'What justifies a conception of justice is not its being true to an order antecedent to and given to us, but its congruence with our deeper understanding of ourselves and our aspirations, and our realization that, *given our history and the traditions embedded in our public life*, it is the most reasonable doctrine *for us*.' "[7] Following Rorty and his Rawls, it would seem that the principles of justice must either be deduced strictly from a transhistorical account of the nature of man or we must affirm our principles simply as our own. But of course this is not really a choice according to Rorty, for only the latter alternative is genuine, the former being a false pretension.

What Rorty implicitly denies by presenting matters this way is the possibility that we might take a genuinely critical stance toward the principles we receive from our communities. Yet in response to this implicit denial or claim, we may raise a couple of questions. First, can we really be satisfied, precisely if we are serious about the principles of justice given to us by our communities, simply to articulate and affirm—as a matter of mere belief—our particular community's understanding of justice? And second, has Rorty given a fair

---

6. "Priority," pp. 179–189. The most important later works of Rawls to which Rorty points are "Justice as Fairness: Political not Metaphysical" and "Kantian Constructivism in Moral Theory" *Journal of Philosophy* 77 (1980): 512–572.

7. "Priority," pp. 179–180, 185. Rorty is quoting from Rawls's "Kantian Constructivism," p. 519. The emphasis is Rorty's.

depiction of the alternatives, especially the supposedly impossible "philosophic" alternative?

Leaving this second question aside for the moment, let us focus on the first. Here we may be helped by a reflection offered by William Galston in an essay entitled "Pluralism and Social Unity."[8] This essay, which is also an interpretation, although a more critical one, of Rawls, implicitly opposes Rorty's view that Rawls's more recent work has made it clear that he was never so "rationalistic" as many supposed. In opposition to Rorty, Galston contends that there has been a shift in Rawls's thought, that is, that Rawls's turn away from a more rigorous theoretical defense of the principles of justice to an articulation of the beliefs already present in our "public culture" is indeed a *turn*. More importantly, though, Galston is critical of this turn. Galston raises a number of objections, but we may focus on what seem to be the broadest and most powerful.

The line of thought in question begins with the following objection to Rawls's more recent approach. "By asking us to separate general truth claims from the elucidation of our shared understandings," Galston objects, "[this approach] *distorts the deepest meaning of those understandings.*"[9] What Galston means by this brief remark (which, we should note, would apply not only to Rawls but also to the many others today who share his presuppositions) is something like this: as soon as one attempts simply to articulate and describe our beliefs as nothing more than "our" beliefs, that is, as *mere* beliefs, one necessarily fails to be true to the beliefs themselves, at least by failing to capture or attend to the way we experience these beliefs. For when we believe something, to put it as plainly as possible, we believe that it is *true*. "When Americans say," to take Galston's example, "that all human beings are created equal and endowed with certain unalienable rights, they intend this not as a description of their own convictions but, rather, as universal truths, valid everywhere and binding on all." Galston extends this into a fur-

---

8. "Pluralism and Social Unity," found in *Liberal Purposes* (Cambridge: Cambridge University Press, 1991), pp. 140–162. Galston also has another helpful statement on more or less this same question of the movement away from "objectivism" in contemporary theory: "Pierce's Cable and Plato's Cave: Objectivity and Community in Contemporary Political Philosophy" *Liberal Purposes*, pp. 22–41.

9. Galston, p. 158. Emphasis added.

ther, related objection: "Indeed, that claim [the claim to universal truth] is at the heart of their normative force. If our principles are valid for us only because we (happen to) believe them, then they are not binding even for us." "The reason is straightforward," according to Galston: "If someone argues that we ought to do something because it corresponds to the best interpretation of the shared understandings that constitute our culture, it is always open to me to ask why I should consider myself bound by those understandings."[10] To put this another way, principles of justice, in order to truly obligate us, must have the support of more than mere cultural or communal acceptance, for otherwise nothing can be said in response to that individual who is willing to question his community and who asks whether he should be bound by justice. This latter objection is particularly pertinent as an objection to Rawls, for Rawls is famous for the contention that the right is prior to the good. That is, Rawls maintains that we are obligated to obey the dictates of right even when they come into conflict (as he grants they sometimes might) with our own good or even with the good of "society as a whole." But is it enough to defend such a powerful obligation merely to insist that we are obligated because such a conviction is one of our cultural or communal beliefs about justice? Can this response put to rest the doubts and questions that inevitably arise, not only in the minds of "foundationalists" seeking a standard beyond "our" community, but in any sensitive and thoughtful moral life? Is it merely as the products of a misguided philosophic tradition, rather than as morally serious citizens who have always been concerned with the question of the true demands of justice, that we require more of our convictions—and inevitably claim more for them—than that they are "ours"?[11]

---

10. Galston, p. 158.

11. It is worth noting that even Rorty himself speaks at times in terms that suggest a transhistorical standard of judgment. For instance, even when arguing that "the liberal societies of our century have produced more and more people who are able to recognize the contingency of the language in which they state their highest hopes—the contingency of their own consciences. . . . ," Rorty claims that "such recognition is *the chief virtue* of the members of a liberal society," and "the culture of such a society *should* aim at curing us of our 'deep metaphysical need'"; moreover, he approves of the view that would understand the difference between those who "realize" the contingency of their convictions and those who do not as the dif-

Now, if we share Galston's dissatisfaction with simply articulating our beliefs as mere beliefs, what alternative do we have? Perhaps we could return to the original Rawls. By faulting Rawls for the turn he has taken, Galston implies that Rawls would have been better off sticking to his older approach. Indeed, Galston tells us that *A Theory of Justice* was first received so favorably because it restored the hope of non-relativistic judgment, or because it responded to the felt need for a non-relativistic basis of legitimate "political evaluation."[12] If there is a relativist Rawls (championed by Rorty), there is also—or at least there seems to have been originally—a rationalist Rawls. Rather than turning to this Rawls, however, I will argue that we are ultimately better served by turning to Plato; and I will contend, in connection with this, that Plato has been dismissed by Rorty and those in general agreement with him on the basis of a distorted view of Plato's true approach. In order to begin to explain and defend these claims, though, I want to approach Plato indirectly, by way of a path that is at least somewhat more familiar within contemporary political theory: Kant.

Why Kant? In the first place, Kant is the philosopher we would eventually come to, I believe, if we worked our way through the early Rawls. In the preface to *A Theory of Justice* Rawls himself presents his theory as "highly Kantian in nature,"[13] and in the body of the work he borrows certain essential principles from Kant, the most important of which I have already alluded to: the priority of the right over the good is an adaptation of Kant's insistence on the primacy of moral duty.[14] Yet, even if we focus on just this one key principle, we can see that Rawls—even the early, more rationalist Rawls—borrows from Kant without following the rigor of his arguments. It is revealing to consider just how far Rawls is from according the prior-

---

ference between the "civilized" and the "barbarian" ("The Contingency of a Liberal Community," pp. 46–47, emphasis added). Similarly, Rorty often and emphatically speaks of "progress," which is presumably change for the better and not just change from one historical situation to another (see, e.g., "Priority," pp. 193–196).

12. Galston, p. 155.

13. *A Theory of Justice* (Cambridge: Harvard University Press, 1971), p. viii.

14. See especially *A Theory of Justice*, pp. 31–32. Also very helpful on this connection between Rawls and Kant, and more generally on the meaning of the priority of the right over the good, is Michael Sandel's *Liberalism and the Limits of Justice* (Cambridge: Cambridge University Press, 1982), especially pp. 1–14.

ity of the right over the good the same meaning and power that Kant accorded the primacy of moral duty. Although he opens *A Theory of Justice* by laying out a set of propositions that "seem to express our intuitive conviction of the primacy of justice" (propositions such as "laws and institutions no matter how efficient and well-arranged must be reformed or abolished if they are unjust" and "an injustice is tolerable only when it is necessary to avoid an even greater injustice"), Rawls softens or qualifies himself in his very next breath: "No doubt [these propositions] are expressed too strongly."[15] More important, though, than Rawls's hesitancy to unequivocally proclaim the priority of the right over the good is that he does not go to Kant's lengths to examine the implications of this claim and to defend its possibility. Rawls includes the priority of the right over the good as a feature of his theory to be maintained, like all its features, only to the extent that we find it "intuitively appealing," "attractive," and "workable."[16] Hence Rawls will appeal to the priority of the right over the good when he needs to supplement the emphasis on self-interest in his doctrine,[17] but he does not make its demands the focal point of his thought. As a result, we find Rawls willing to shy away from the rigor of Kant by rejecting Kantian universality, for example, or by making a closely connected effort to maintain categorical imperatives without fully divorcing them from the empirical ends of human desire. In a remarkable section of *A Theory of Justice*, Rawls describes his theory as an attempt to adopt Kant's notions of autonomy and duty while discarding Kant's emphasis on universality and his insistence that our natural desires or inclinations are unfit to serve as a basis for moral laws.[18] From a truly Kantian point of view, however, this is to try to have the fruit without the tree, for, according to Kant, it is only through our capacity to set and adhere to universal law that we realize our autonomy, and it is only by transcending the empirical ends sought by our inclinations that categorical imperatives become truly categorical; without this foundation, duty cannot preserve its independence from the merely hypothetical maxims of

---

15. *A Theory of Justice*, pp. 3–4.
16. See especially *A Theory of Justice*, pp. 48–50.
17. See, for instance, *A Theory of Justice*, pp. 101–102, 145, 148.
18. Section 40, "The Kantian Interpretation of Justice as Fairness," pp. 251–257.

prudence which are contingent on an end other than duty itself.[19] These differences between Rawls and Kant are reflections, ultimately, of a more general one, traceable to a difference of purpose: because Rawls seeks to present an "attractive" theory of justice that will serve the interests of certain disadvantaged groups in society and will enlist wide support in that cause, he is not as eager as Kant to dwell on the more severe and demanding aspects of morality and to press the difficult questions these raise. One could never say of *A Theory of Justice*, as Kant does of his *Groundwork of the Metaphysic of Morals*, that its "sole aim . . . is to seek out and establish *the supreme principle of morality;*"[20] this is not to deny, though, that Rawls's theory relies on "Kantian" obligations even as it fails to repeat, and even undoes, the work of Kant.

What we find in Kant, then, which Rawls, for all his claims to Kantianism, avoids, is a rigorous and direct *examination* of morality. Rather than seeking merely to articulate our basic convictions about morality, or rather than trying to defend these convictions by moderating them to fit comfortably within a larger system aimed at social reform, Kant made it his first and primary task to *analyze* morality on its most immediate moral level. Now, this difference between Kant and Rawls, important in its own right, is of particular interest to us for a further reason: it marks a similarity, at least if posed in general terms, *between Kant and Plato*—one that they share over

---

19. See especially Kant, *Critique of Practical Reason*, trans. by Lewis White Beck (Indianapolis: The Bobbs-Merrill Company, 1956), pp. 18–19, 28–49, 72–73, 89, and *Groundwork of the Metaphysic of Morals*, trans. by H. J. Paton (New York: Harper Torchbooks, 1964), pp. 74–79, 82–94, 108–113. In *Liberalism and the Limits of Justice* Sandel points to the following passage from Kant's *Groundwork* as particulary indicative of the difference between Kant and Rawls: " '*Empirical principles* are always unfitted to serve as a ground for moral laws. The universality with which these laws should hold for all rational beings without exception—the unconditioned practical necessity which they thus impose—falls away if their basis is taken from the *special constitution of human nature* or from the accidental circumstances in which it is placed' " (p. 36; the emphasis is Kant's). More generally, Sandel's argument is helpful in bringing out the half-heartedness of Rawls's Kantianism (see especially pp. 35–40). On this same issue, see also Allan Bloom, *Giants and Dwarfs* (New York: Simon and Schuster, 1990), pp. 331–334.

20. *Groundwork*, p. 60. The emphasis is Kant's. Regarding the difference between Rawls's intention and Kant's, see also *Groundwork*, pp. 77–78.

and against contemporary political theory. Broadly stated, Kant and Plato share a primary emphasis on thinking through the most basic questions of morality. And it is ultimately this broad or basic similarity—a similarity Kant himself acknowledges precisely by setting his own analysis of morality in opposition to the conclusions the ancient philosophers drew, i.e., by understanding the ancients as among his chief opponents[21]—that makes Kant such an instructive way of approaching Plato, for it provides the ground of a fundamental and revealing disagreement.

Before turning to look at the disagreement between Kant and Plato, however, or rather as a way of leading into this, I want to underline two often overlooked or misunderstood features of ancient thought. (These features apply to ancient thought in general, or at least to Aristotle as well as to Plato, but of course my primary concern here is with Plato.) The first returns us to our earlier question of whether Rorty gives a fair account of all traditional philosophy when he portrays it as unanimously "foundationalist." For although the view that includes the ancients as the original foundationalists has come to be widely accepted, it is in fact a misconception or at least badly misleading. The picture, not to say the caricature, drawn by the likes of Rorty and Walzer, in which the ancients are depicted as fleeing from the contingency of ordinary life in search of some transcendent standard of judgment, misrepresents the true character of ancient political philosophy: it would be much less of an exaggeration to say that the ancient approach, at least subsequent to its most important change in orientation, the "Socratic turn," is defined precisely by its *refusal* to begin by seeking some vantage point beyond the convictions and opinions of ordinary political life. The ancient approach, characteristic of Plato's Socrates in particular, is to argue *dialectically*, which means that the ancients begin by taking most seriously—if not accepting uncritically—the most basic opinions present in our everyday understanding of justice or morality.[22] The fail-

---

21. See *Groundwork*, pp. 61, 72, and *Critique of Practical Reason*, pp. 66–67.

22. At this point someone might object—surely Rorty would—that there is a problem in speaking of "our everyday understanding of justice or morality" because the understanding from which the ancients began was a pre-modern Greek understanding and therefore not the same as "ours." (Consider especially Rorty's note 34 to "The Priority of Democracy to Philosophy.") Against this objection, I would

ure to appreciate this feature of the ancient approach may be connected with the second misconception about ancient thought: it is often argued that the ancients, in contrast especially to Kant, begin from a view of the human good from which they then derive the principles of virtue. In other words, the ancients are thought to begin from happiness or "flourishing," not from duty.[23] This too, it seems to me, is mistaken. By beginning from ordinary opinions, the ancients begin by understanding justice in particular as a matter of obligation, or of duty, of what we "owe" to others or to our commu-

---

make only a brief observation in defense of the continued relevance of the ancients. If one looks at the opinions from which the ancients begin—that is, if one simply opens their books with no preconceptions about what they contain—one finds that these opinions are so basic and fundamental that it is hard to imagine any "historical morality" not including them in some form or another, or even any person who is not in some way moved by them. For instance, as much as we may be the products of a universalistic and individualistic modern liberalism, the opinion expressed early in Plato's *Republic* that justice is helping friends and harming enemies, or in other words, that we ought to be loyal to our community and to contribute to the good of this larger whole, makes immediate sense to us. Indeed, not only is this opinion essentially *the* theme of the recent rise of communitarianism, but more simply, we still admire in our everyday lives people who sacrifice for the "common good"—we even speak, for instance, of a duty to "give something back to the community"—and we fault those who show no regard for any end beyond themselves. (As for "harming enemies," although we are less eager to regard this as a part of justice, we still live in political communities that go to war and thus rightly require—as most of us would acknowledge—such service from their members.) Or, to give another example, we can grasp immediately what Aristotle means when he speaks of the unjust man as the one who unfairly seizes more than his due share (see Rawls' reference to Aristotle in *A Theory of Justice*, p. 10).

23. For a sense of the wide range of scholars who hold some version of this view, consider Julia Annas, *The Morality of Happiness* (New York: Oxford University Press, 1993); G. E. M. Anscombe, "Modern Moral Philosophy" *Philosophy* 33 (1958): 1–19; Stephen Salkever, "Virtue, Obligation and Politics" *American Political Science Review* 68 (1974): 78–92; and Martha Nussbaum, "Non- Relative Virtues: An Aristotelian Approach" *Midwest Studies in Philosophy*, Volume 13, ed. by Peter French, Theodore Uehling, Jr., and Howard Wettstein (South Bend: University of Notre Dame Press, 1988): 32–53. Recently, this view has been expounded especially by proponents of what has come to be known as "virtue-ethics." I have been helped by a discussion of the rise of "virtue-ethics" (a trend associated particularly with the interpretation of Aristotle) in an unpublished doctoral dissertation by Susan Collins, "The Ends of Action: The Moral Virtues in Aristotle's *Nicomachean Ethics*" (Boston College, 1994), pp. 4–8.

nities. In this respect, the ancients are not as far from Kant as they are frequently assumed to be.[24]

Of course, Kant's opposition to the ancients indicates that if the ancients begin from the primacy of duty, they may not simply stay there. The disagreement between Kant and the ancients, at least if we begin from Kant's presentation of it, hinges above all on this question. Kant presents his own examination of morality as the most thoroughgoing defense of duty possible. He alone, he insists, does full justice to the demands implicit in our ordinary understanding of morality. Kant claims, in other words, to differ from the ancients in listening more attentively to the true voice of virtue—a voice that, he insists, proclaims virtue to be an end higher than any other and that demands unconditional obedience. Kant's moral teaching can thus be understood as an attempt to isolate a few closely connected thoughts that form the bedrock of morality as it is known to our "ordinary reason." To summarize briefly, the first of these thoughts is the concept, or the "Idea," of the absolute value of the good will, that is, of the good will as the only good that can be conceived of as good for its own sake and not for any further purpose that it might achieve. The *intention* behind moral action, the will from which it springs, must therefore be regarded as its highest aspect according to Kant. Second, moral action must be understood as *morally obligatory*. Putting these thoughts together, Kant argues that an action is truly moral only if it is performed, not merely in accordance with duty, but *from duty*, that is, out of a good will determined directly by the moral law. While apparently moral actions, in other words, may have any num-

---

24. My claim here might seem to be contradicted by the first book of Aristotle's *Nicomachean Ethics*, since Aristotle begins his treatment of the human good with a discussion of happiness. However, contrary to what Book One might lead some readers to anticipate, in his subsequent treatment of the moral virtues (in Books Two through Five), Aristotle does not derive the virtues or their demands from a prior notion of happiness. Instead, he treats the moral virtues on their own terms, stressing that they are to be understood as ends in themselves, performed for their own sake, not as subordinate to any other end they might serve. See, for example, *Nicomachean Ethics* 1105a28–b9, 1115b20–24, 1122b6–7, and 1145a4–6. On the difference between the view of "virtue-ethicists" and Aristotle's genuine approach, see also Peter Simpson, "Contemporary Virtue Ethics and Aristotle," *Review of Metaphysics* 45 (1992): 503–524, and Susan Collins, "The Ends of Action," pp. 4–11.

ber of motives—one might refrain from lying, say, out of a calculated regard for one's reputation and credit—Kant insists that genuinely moral action must have a distinctive motive of its own; the various species of self-regard, in particular, must be replaced by "reverence for the moral law." What is to guide moral action, then, is not the result or consequence to be accomplished by this or that action, but simply the moral law itself, given its form, according to Kant, by the categorical imperative (the only truly binding imperative, or the only true law): "Act only on that maxim through which you can at the same time will that it should become a universal law."[25]

Kant insists, to repeat, that all this is implicit in our ordinary understanding of morality, in what he sometimes calls "the ordinary reason of mankind." But he also notes that special efforts are required to preserve the "purity" of morality. To grasp what he means by this, we must consider what Kant sees as the threat to morality's purity. In general terms, Kant is concerned with keeping morality pure of empirical ends whose contingency would qualify the moral law, thereby destroying its status as law and its basis in an unconditional good. More simply, however, the most important of such ends—and the one that in a sense incorporates all the others—is *happiness*. Happiness, as well as the faculty or "virtue" by which we pursue it, the "skill in the choice of the means to one's own greatest well-being," namely, prudence, is *the* rival to morality, according to Kant. What Kant means by the primacy of moral duty is above all its superiority to each individual's prudent regard for his own good. Only by transcending our concern to secure our own advantage can our moral actions attain their distinctive non-mercenary character, with our virtue truly distinguishable from vice, and can we thus become "worthy of happiness."[26] Now, it is true that Kant may seem

---

25. See especially *Groundwork*, pp. 61–71, 74–98; *Critique of Practical Reason*, pp. 17–42, 74–92; "On the Common Saying: 'This May be True in Theory, but it does not Apply in Practice,'" found in *Kant's Political Writings*, ed. by Hans Reiss, trans. by H. B. Nisbet (Cambridge: Cambridge University Press, 1991), pp. 66-72.

26. Consider: "*Empirical principles* are always unfitted to serve as a ground for moral laws. . . . The principle of *personal happiness* is, however, the most objectionable, not merely because it is false and its pretense that well-being always adjusts itself to well-doing is contradicted by experience; nor merely because it contributes nothing whatever towards establishing morality, since making a man happy is quite

at times to back off from a hard-line insistence on the subordination of happiness. It is true that Kant does give some place not only to the demand that we become "*worthy* of happiness" but also to the other concern this formulation implies or at least points to—that is, that our worthiness should receive its due, or that we should actually *be happy.* If Kant clings, in other words, to that aspect of our ordinary notion of morality that insists moral worth is the one thing essential and unconditionally praiseworthy, he is not simply deaf to that other aspect that longs to see moral worth coincide with or be rewarded by happiness. In fact, Kant even goes so far as to defend the postulation of the existence of God and a future life in order to respond to our hope for happiness, or, perhaps better, in order to preserve the possibility of the "highest good" at which our moral strivings aim, a good that requires that virtue, the "supreme" but not yet "perfect" good, be met with proportionate happiness.[27] Nevertheless, Kant insists that happiness, undeniably important as it may be, must remain subordinate to the moral law, neither qualifying its demands nor corrupting the motives of its adherents. Even when arguing for the postulation of the existence of God, Kant goes out of his way to stress the primacy of morality: "The moral law . . . obligates us all by itself, independently of any purpose whatever as material condition."[28]

---

different from making him good and making him prudent or astute in seeking his advantage quite different from making him virtuous; but because it bases morality on sensuous motives which rather undermine it and totally destroy its sublimity, inasmuch as the motives of virtue are put in the same class as those of vice and we are instructed only to become better at calculation, the specific difference between virtue and vice being completely wiped out" (*Groundwork*, pp. 109–110, the emphasis is Kant's). See also *Groundwork*, pp. 63, 65–71, 74–75, 83–85, 104–112; *Critique of Practical Reason*, pp. 35–38, 63–64, 74–86, 96–97; "Theory and Practice," pp. 66–72.

27. See *Critique of Practical Reason*, pp. 116–138; *Critique of Judgment*, trans. by Werner S. Pluhar (Indianapolis: Hackett Publishing Co., 1987), pp. 336–353; *Critique of Pure Reason*, trans. by Norman Kemp Smith (New York: St. Martin's Press, 1965), A804/B832–A832/B860; "Theory and Practice," pp. 65–66. In these sections, Kant acknowledges that the postulation of God and a future life is a response to the problem that, without such support, it would be unrealistic and contrary to our experience to expect a necessary connection between virtue and happiness.

28. *Critique of Judgment*, p. 339. Consider also: "This proof [the moral proof of the existence of God], to which we could easily give the form of logical precision,

But is Kant right about morality? Are its demands really what he says they are? A return to Plato, I think, is one of the best ways of pursuing this question, for Plato takes up the same fundamental questions as Kant, yet presents the decisive alternative to Kant. Plato ultimately defends a position that is in opposition to Kant's, but he does so in a way that begins from the same concerns and starting point as Kant. Now, as for why Plato is led in a different direction from Kant and what his own view is, it would be a mistake to try to say anything conclusive here, since that is the task of the body of this study. Besides, if there is one thing that can be said with certainty about Plato's view, it is that it is difficult to say what it is; it is hard to grasp and even more difficult to summarize than Kant's. Still, I should say a few words indicating at least what I understand to be the outlines of this view, and also indicating where Plato diverges from Kant. To do so, I begin from a point that may help to explain the greater difficulty of giving a simple statement of what Plato's view is: it is less clear in Plato just what morality, or justice (as he speaks of it),[29] consists of or demands. Plato, as I will try to show in

---

is not trying to say that it is as necessary to assume that God exists as it is to acknowledge that the moral law is valid, so that anyone who cannot convince himself that God exists may judge himself released from the obligations that the moral law imposes. No!"; and again: "Nor is the argument meant to say that it is necessary *for morality* that we assume that the happiness of all rational beings in the world is [to be] proportionate to their morality, but rather that *morality makes* it necessary for us to make this assumption" (*Critique of Judgment*, p. 340, the emphasis is Kant's). It is true that Kant has several statements that suggest that morality requires the existence of God in a stronger sense—that is, that the obligatory status of morality *would be* cast into doubt without this support. See *Critique of Pure Reason*, A811/B839, A812–813/B840–841, A815/B843, A828/B856, *Critique of Practical Reason*, p. 120. However, these more radical statements, as striking as they are, must be weighed not only against those quoted above but against many others that express essentially the same point. For examples (sometimes even within the same section as the more radical statements), see *Critique of Pure Reason*, A807–808/B834–835, A809/B837, A813/B841; *Critique of Practical Reason*, pp. 125, 132, 135, 136; *Critique of Judgment*, p. 341, "Theory and Practice," pp. 65–66.

29. That Plato speaks of "justice" (*dikaiosunē*) as the closest parallel to what Kant calls "morality" is a less significant difference than it might initially appear to be. After all, we must bear in mind that Plato begins by understanding justice as a matter of duty; that is, he approaches the question by considering how each individual is *obligated* to act. Moreover, justice is said to be a virtue in Plato, sometimes

this study, is less certain than Kant that morality or justice can be expressed definitely and simply in terms of universal and absolutely binding rules, that is, in categorical imperatives or unconditional laws. For especially when following such a rule is harmful (say, to take an extreme case, when it would risk the destruction of one's community), it is not clear, to say the least, that adhering to it is what justice bids—and hence it is not clear that the meaning or content of justice can be exhausted by any such rules. Moreover, as further reflection on the implications of points like this will reveal, we do indeed (ultimately) find in Plato a greater emphasis on the good, or happiness, than we find in Kant (who, again, acknowledges the importance of happiness but insists that it must remain subordinate to the demands of morality). One of the reasons that it is harder to say with certainty what Plato thinks justice is, or one of the reasons he is less confident that it can be expressed in categorical demands, is that Plato seems to place great weight on the observation that, as much as we may ordinarily take justice to consist in fixed rules, we also insist that justice must be something good; we thus recognize the importance of the goodness of justice even in our very understanding of what justice is. Again, this has the result that Plato would likely disagree with the implications of Kant's stricter separation of duty and advantage: "What duty is," writes Kant, "is plain of itself to everyone, but what is to bring true, lasting advantage to our whole existence is veiled in impenetrable obscurity."[30] If Plato would perhaps deny that it is so impossible to discern what is advantageous, more important is that he would be skeptical that duty is such a sim-

---

even "human virtue" simply (see especially *Republic* 335c4–5; compare, e.g., Kant, *Groundwork*, pp. 61, 110). The difference in terminology does, however, indicate something of the greater "politicalness" of Plato's approach, which does not separate morality from politics as strictly as Kant's does. As for why Plato would be skeptical of such a separation, perhaps this can be understood in light of the broader disagreement between him and Kant that I try to sketch in the remainder of the present paragraph in the text. On this point, see also Arthur Melzer *The Natural Goodness of Man* (Chicago: University of Chicago Press), p. 131, n. 25.

30. *Critique of Practical Reason*, p. 38. Kant continues "But the moral law commands the most unhesitating obedience from everyone; consequently, the decision as to what is to be done in accordance with it must not be so difficult that even the commonest and most unpracticed understanding without any worldly prudence should go wrong in making it." Contrast especially *Republic* 336a9–338a3.

ple matter. Precisely our concern for the goodness of justice, by making us open to qualifications and revisions in our understanding of what justice is, calls into question what we may originally take to be the simple, categorical demands of justice. To be sure, this poses a problem or indicates a contradiction in our ordinary understanding of justice. But this, in turn, proves to be one of the crucial results of the examination of justice Plato presents Socrates carrying out in the *Republic*: our ordinary understanding of justice, rather than providing a simple touchstone as it does at the foundation of Kant's thought, is shown to be contradictory and in need of improvement.[31]

Now, this leads in the *Republic* to a search for a higher or truer understanding of justice that is not contradictory—an ascent, we might say, to a higher and less confused morality. I began this introduction by speaking of the remarkable conclusions that the *Republic* culminates in, perhaps the most extraordinary of which is that philosophy itself is ultimately declared to be the highest practice of justice, and the philosopher, the one whose soul is in the best order, is said to be the most just man. This conclusion, like the others I alluded to, is at once alluring and perplexing: It sounds very attractive, but how can this be justice? It is especially perplexing, however, if one begins by asserting that this is Plato's view of justice and by trying to make immediate sense of it. Rather than looking directly into the sun, so to speak, I suggest that it makes more sense to attend to the ground and follow Plato in doing the less glamorous but still essential work of examining our ordinary understanding of justice, beginning with the simple question, posed so directly at the outset of Book One of the *Republic,* "What is justice?" This study, then, is meant as a preliminary work, as an investigation of the beginning of the path that leads to Plato's full understanding of justice.

---

31. Again, contrast Kant, this time commenting on the fallibility of philosophy: "Might it not then be more advisable in moral questions to abide by the judgment of ordinary reason and, at the most, to bring in philosophy only in order to set forth the system of morals more fully and intelligibly and to present its rules in a form more convenient for use (though still more so for disputation)—but not in order to lead ordinary human intelligence away from its happy simplicity in respect of human action and to set it by means of philosophy on a new path of enquiry and instruction?" (*Groundwork*, p. 72). See also *Critique of Pure Reason*, A807/B835, A831/B859.

Chapter 1

The Opening of the Question of Justice: Socrates' Exchanges with Cephalus and Polemarchus

I have already indicated some of the reasons for focusing on the beginning of the *Republic*. A further word is in order, however, about this choice and about the character of the passages I will be discussing. Justice is, of course, a theme throughout not only the whole *Republic* but many, not to say all, of Plato's works. Indeed, from a sweeping glance at Plato's dialogues, one gets the impression that there is nothing else to which Plato and his hero, Socrates, devoted more thought and attention. However, it is only in the *Republic*, and especially at its outset, that Plato presents Socrates explicitly taking up and pursuing the most basic question of justice, the question, "What is justice?" To get a sense of Socrates' special interest in justice at the beginning of the *Republic*, we may observe that although Socrates has to be (somewhat playfully) compelled to join the conversation of the Republic (see 327b2–328b3), once the conversation begins, he is the one who directs the others to the question of justice, concentrating particular attention on this one of a number of questions that the preceding discussion might have raised (consider 331c1–9 in context).[1] Moreover, once the question of justice has been taken up, Socrates encourages his company to seek its

---

1. Unless otherwise noted, all references given in parentheses in the text are to the *Republic*. I have used Burnet's Oxford text in *Platonis Opera*, Volume IV. Translations from the Greek are my own.

19

answer rigorously. He does not let the question drop, for instance, when a certain view of justice has been rejected, but rather he urges his company to propose a better view (336a9–10). Socrates' eagerness to pursue the question of justice at the beginning of the *Republic* thus goes together, it seems, with an insistence that the question be neither settled nor abandoned too easily. And if this means that Socrates must play the critic of justice (as it is ordinarily understood) when combating Cephalus and Polemarchus' acceptance of overly simple opinions about what justice is, so too he will play the defender of justice to combat Thrasymachus' brash dismissal of justice as bad for the just man. To sum up the point, then, Socrates' interest in justice at the beginning of the *Republic* is not so much in pressing a certain view of justice, which would likely result in presenting justice as something simpler than it is, as it is in bringing out the full complexity of justice as a question or a problem.

This has a bearing on how we should go about reading the beginning of the *Republic*. The beginning of the *Republic* is a model of Platonic writing, in which Plato presents us not with a systematic, step-by-step defense of a certain teaching but with something more like an invitation or a challenge. There have been a number of very helpful discussions of how to read Plato's dialogues, and I do not wish here to recapitulate all of their intricate guidelines.[2] But it is worth highlighting what I take to be the most important point and the one most relevant to our present task. It can be stated as a maxim: Plato cannot be understood passively. Despite all the undeni-

---

2. See Jacob Klein, *A Commentary on Plato's Meno* (Chapel Hill: University of North Carolina Press, 1965), pp. 3–31; Leo Strauss, *The City and Man* (Chicago: University of Chicago Press, 1964), pp. 50–62, and "On a New Interpretation of Plato's Political Philosophy" *Social Research* 13 (1946): 326–367, especially pp. 348–352; Alfarabi, "Plato's *Laws*" in *Medieval Political Philosophy*, ed. by Ralph Lerner and Mushin Mahdi (Ithaca: Cornell University Press, 1972), especially pp. 84–85; Friedrich Schleiermacher, *Introductions to the Dialogues of Plato*, trans. by William Dobson (New York: Arno Press, 1973), pp. 17–18; David Bolotin, "The Life of Philosophy and the Immortality of the Soul: An Introduction to Plato's *Phaedo*" *Ancient Philosophy* 7 (1987): 39–56, especially pp. 39–41, and *Plato's Dialogue on Friendship* (Ithaca: Cornell University Press, 1979), pp. 12–13; Peter Ahrensdorf, *The Death of Socrates and the Life of Philosophy* (Albany: State University of New York Press, 1995), pp. 3–7; John Sallis, *Being and Logos* (New York: Humanities Press International, 1986), pp. 1–6.

able beauty of Plato's dialogues, they are in fact riddled with all kinds of difficulties and puzzles: poor arguments, strange shifts, sometimes even downright contradictions (and these by Socrates *himself*, not only by his interlocutors). Unless we assume, however, that Socrates and Plato were extremely careless and foolish, these apparent blunders should be the sparks of our thought. *Why*, for example, does Socrates separate justice and wisdom just moments after conjoining them and just moments before (implicitly) reuniting them (compare 351b6–e1 with 349b1–350c11 and then 353e7– 354a9)? *Why* does he first portray artisans and rulers as selfless and then later stress their concern for wages (compare 341c4–342e11 with 345e5– 347a6)? Questions such as these, more than any obvious "thesis" Socrates might seem to promote or defend, provide the best way of approaching the task of uncovering Socrates' true understanding of justice and of making our way through the twists and turns of Plato's text. Without further delay, then, let us turn to that task.

Socrates' Objection to Cephalus' View of Justice (328b4–331d3)

The conversation about justice in the *Republic* does not begin immediately, although justice is surely a theme of the drama from the very opening scene: Socrates and his companion Glaucon, on their way back from a sacred festival in the Piraeus (the Athenian port), are intercepted and forced to join a group of young men because they lack the strength necessary to resist (327a1–328b3). The explicit discussion of justice, however, begins with Socrates' objection to the view of justice held by Cephalus, the head of the household in which the conversation of the *Republic* takes place. Against Cephalus' view that justice is simply telling the truth and returning what one has taken (or received: *labēi*) from another, Socrates asks whether justice is not more complicated, that is, whether it is not in fact only sometimes just to do these things, but other times unjust (331c1–5). Socrates' well-known example is of a man faced with the demand that weapons he had been keeping for a friend be returned when his friend is in a fit of rage. "I suppose," Socrates says, "that all would say . . . that one ought not to return such things, that the man who did return them would not be just, and, further, that one ought not to be willing to tell the truth in all respects to someone in such a state" (331c5–9). Cephalus promptly concedes Socrates' point, placing himself among the "all" who would presumably agree that such a case would justify deviating from the rule. And in light of Cephalus' concession, Socrates concludes that telling the truth and returning what one has taken, Cephalus' definition of justice, is not the true definition (*horos*) of justice (331d1–3).

But I should be more precise: Cephalus never offered a definition of justice. Telling the truth and returning what one has taken is a definition of justice formulated by Socrates not by Cephalus—formulated, however, by articulating what was implicit in other things Cephalus had said. Let us take a brief look back, then, and see how Socrates arrived at this definition of justice that he attributes to Cephalus.

After arriving at Cephalus' home and finding him returned from his sacrifices and seated so as to be the center of attention (328b8–c4), Socrates had questioned Cephalus about two things, perhaps the only two in which Cephalus' firsthand experience might be thought to make him more of an expert than Socrates: old age and wealth. Alluding only indirectly to the fears Cephalus might have of death (328e5–6), Socrates asked him whether he had good things or bad things to report about old age, whether it is rough and troublesome or easy and gentle (328d7–e7). This gave Cephalus a chance to do a little boasting. For, according to his report, old age is difficult for those who mourn the loss of the pleasures of youth, but for orderly and good-natured sorts like himself, old age offers a welcome relief from the strain of wild and mad desires—or, at any rate, old age is not such a burden (329a1–d6, compare c5–d1 with d4–6 and 328d2–4). It was in response to Cephalus' claim about the importance of character that Socrates then brought up wealth. For he "supposed" that "the many" would not accept Cephalus' claim that his character is responsible for the ease with which he bears old age but would point to his wealth instead: "For they say that for the wealthy there are many consolations" (329d7–e5). Cephalus granted that there was something to this objection, but would only go so far: wealth and character are both necessary; neither is sufficient without the other (329e6–330a6). But when Socrates pressed the topic of wealth and asked Cephalus what he regarded as the greatest good he had gained from being so wealthy, Cephalus' reply could be seen as a further concession to the many's claim that it is wealth that most of all helps him in his old age, even if it helps him in a way the many would not have had in mind. For according to Cephalus the greatest good that comes from the possession of wealth is not the material comfort it brings in old age (or at any age) but the relief it brings from the fears that torment the old. When a man reaches the point at which he realizes that he will soon meet his end, Cephalus said, he begins to fear that there might be some truth to the tales he had previously laughed at, the tales that punishments in Hades await those who have committed injustices here (330d4–e2). Now, Cephalus expressed some uncertainty as to whether the increased respect for these tales is due to the debility of old age or to the special insight the old may have into the things in Hades because they are already closer to them (330e2–4). But Cephalus' lingering doubts have not kept him from trying to protect himself. And his speech contrasting a man secure in his own justice with one tormented by fears (330e6ff.), together with his own urgent sacrificing (328c2, 331d7–9) and his implicit admission that he spent his youth pursuing the pleasures of the body (cf. 328d2–4 with 329c5–d1), indicates that he is worried about his own fate.[3] So Cephalus answered that his wealth is most useful for keeping him from doing injustice and for settling his debts: "For avoiding the compulsion to cheat someone or to lie, and for not leaving to go there [sc. Hades] all afraid because one owes some sacrifices to a god or money to a human being, for this the possession of money contributes a great share. It has many other uses. But one thing against another, I set this down as not the least thing, Socrates, for which wealth is very useful for an intelligent man" (331b1–8).

It was from this statement that Socrates took the definition of justice as telling the truth and returning what one has taken, articulating as a rule the view implicit in what Cephalus had said (331c1–3). Yet, while this definition surely is not a misrepresentation of what Cephalus thinks justice is, it is easy to see that Socrates' procedure abstracts from, or ignores, much of what Cephalus had talked

---

3. Contrast the testimony of Cephalus' deeds with the more unambiguous judgments of his lifelong virtue offered by R. C. Cross and A. D. Woozely, *Plato's Republic: A Philosophical Commentary* (New York: St. Martin's Press, 1964), p. 2, and C. D. C. Reeve, *Philosopher-Kings* (Princeton: Princeton University Press, 1988), pp. 6–7.

about. Most obviously, Socrates makes no mention of the sacrifices owed to the gods, or indeed of piety and the gods at all. Whereas Cephalus had just spoken of justice and piety (see also 331a4: *dikaiōs kai hosiōs*), Socrates seems to take up only justice and to ignore piety. And by ignoring piety and the gods, Socrates ignores the support Cephalus thinks there at least might be for justice. Cephalus' hopes and fears about divine justice in Hades provide the incentive for his justice here on earth. However, as this fact itself suggests, it is possible that Socrates, in limiting his explicit attention to justice, does not simply forget about piety as he appears to, for justice and piety are related. Indeed, in the *Euthyphro*, Socrates goes so far as to suggest that piety might be a part of justice, however that might ultimately have to be understood.[4] So even though Socrates appears to leave piety out of the discussion, we should keep in the back of our minds the question of whether it belongs in the discussion and whether it is not a matter of interest present, as it were, behind the scenes.[5]

At any rate, we can now return to Socrates' objection to the definition of justice he attributes to Cephalus, a definition which, while not explicitly taking account of everything Cephalus had said, at least states the content of justice in terms of two principles that Cephalus evidently considers principles of justice. To repeat, Socrates raises the objection that it is not always just to tell the truth and

---

4. See *Euthyphro* 11eff.; cf. Paul Friedländer, *Plato*, Volume 2, trans. by Hans Meyerhoff (Princeton: Princeton University Press, 1969), p. 53; see also Seth Benardete, *Socrates' Second Sailing* (Chicago: University of Chicago Press, 1989), p. 15.

5. Contrast the considerably different interpretation offered by Darrell Dobbs, who argues that Cephalus' piety is merely a shallow, calculating piety and that true piety comes on stage only with his departure ("The Piety of Thought in Plato's *Republic*, Book 1" *American Political Science Review* 88 (1994): 668–683, especially pp. 670–673). More important than Dobbs's criticism of Cephalus is his characterization of Socrates as pious, that is, as a proponent of what Dobbs describes as a genuinely pious union of "reverence" with "reason" over and against "rationalism" (see also, in particular, pp. 669, 673–674, and 680–681). Without making any assertions of my own here about the ultimate status of Socrates' piety or lack of it, I would only note that in his interpretation of Book One, Dobbs curiously pays much more attention to this question than to the content of Socrates' examination of justice, especially to the more radical aspects of that examination that I will try to bring out in what follows. Stated another way, Dobbs downplays the main topic of the surface of the discussion, or does the exact reverse of Socrates in directing our focus away from justice and toward piety.

return what one has taken, since, as he supposes all would concede, it would not be just to do so in instances such as the one in which one is confronted by a mad friend demanding the return of his weapons. Now, on first hearing, Socrates' objection certainly seems very simple, and it also seems to be something which, as he suggests, anyone would join Cephalus in agreeing with: the rule admits of exceptions. The important question, though, is how such exceptions are to be understood, and how the rule is to be understood in light of such exceptions. For rules seem to provide a clear standard of justice: justice is x, y, and z, in this case telling the truth and returning what one has taken. But, as is indicated by the allowance for exceptions, and by the admission that in the exceptions *the deviation from the rule and not the rule is just*, justice is never thought to be only x, y, and z.[6] As his concession to Socrates shows, Cephalus holds another opinion about justice. Beyond telling the truth and returning what one has taken, he also thinks that justice is not something harmful, or, stated positively, he thinks that it is something good. And indeed this thought appears to be even more important than the rule that justice is telling the truth and returning what one has taken, since it can justify an override of that rule.[7]

By thinking through the acknowledgment, then, that there are exceptions to the rules of justice, we see that this acknowledgment reveals another thought about what justice is, a thought not expressed by any rule, but apparently stronger than any rule. Our own agreement with Socrates' example, it is important to add, shows that the belief that justice is good is not idiosyncratic to Cephalus but belongs to us all. And if we begin to think out the implications of our willingness to sacrifice rules when following them is not good, we may begin to see that this can lead very far. In fact, we might even

---

6. Recall that Socrates stated three things that he supposed all would acknowledge about the weapons example: (1) that one ought not to return such things, (2) *that the man who did return them would not be just*, and (3) that one ought not to be willing to tell the truth in all respects to someone in such a state.

7. Compare Aristotle's *Politics* 3.10, where Aristotle rejects several possible distributions of political authority because they would be bad for the city, including a certain law because "it is clear that it will destroy the city, and yet it is surely not virtue that destroys what possesses it, nor is the just destructive of a city; so it is clear that this law cannot be just" (1280a18–21).

begin to wonder, led by just this first step into the *Republic*, in what way rules can even be the standard of justice, or, to be perhaps less extreme, whether it is not necessary to try to find a rule, or a way of expressing justice, that is never in conflict with justice being good.[8]

Polemarchus' Defense of His Inheritance and the Question of Owed and Fitting (331d4–332c4)

Once Socrates has objected to Cephalus' view of justice, Cephalus leaves quickly. Socrates' objection, by calling into question Cephalus' view of justice, also calls into question what Cephalus had regarded as a straightforward proposition: tell the truth, return what you have taken—also sacrifice to the gods—and, if the tales about Hades are true, at least you can help to protect yourself. Socrates' objection calls this proposition into question since one would not expect the gods to reward or punish on the basis of something that is not in fact justice (see 330d8–e1, 331a4). Of course, it is most likely that Cephalus does not see all the implications of Socrates' argument. But at least we can say that while Cephalus may claim that his old age has brought a newfound love of speeches (328d2–4), he does not seem to care much for arguments, especially ones that call into question what at this point of his life cannot be called into question. With what is probably a nervous laugh, Cephalus readily turns over his side of the argument to his son, Polemarchus (331d6–9). He himself leaves to attend to the sacrifices (or, more generally, the sacred things: *ta hiera*), and we are not told that he returns at any point in the very

---

8. Socrates' opening argument has radical implications. Aware of such implications, Kant tries to avoid this general line of reasoning by denying that the moral law admits of exceptions or qualifications and by insisting on the absolute supremacy of "the rule" over considerations of the sort that might lead to exceptions. Yet, among other difficulties this creates, Kant's attempt requires that he depart from the ordinary moral perspective that he claims is his foundation. For, as Cephalus' (and our) agreement here indicates, it is part of our ordinary moral understanding to acknowledge that there are exceptions to rules, and we are willing—we even feel the need—to bend the dictates of justice when they would lead to destructive consequences. Moreover, to repeat a point made in the text above, we do not understand these instances as departures from justice but rather as examples of its flexibility. Our willingness to transform justice in this manner so as to preserve its goodness reveals a problem in strictly divorcing justice, or the moral law, from considerations of advantage.

long conversation of the *Republic*. Although this is the last we see of Cephalus, we should keep in mind the significance of his departure, of his flight from the critical scrutiny of justice to the performance of pious acts. We should keep this in mind as an alternative to the searching conversation of the rest of the *Republic*, a conversation that also replaces the earlier plans of the group to attend the evening session of the sacred festival in the Piraeus (see 328a1–8).[9]

With Cephalus' departure, Polemarchus assumes his role as heir. In the face of Socrates' rejection of Cephalus' view of justice, Polemarchus takes over his father's position, invoking the authority of the poet Simonides to defend it (331d4–5). According to Polemarchus, Simonides said that it is just to give to each what is owed, and Polemarchus is impressed by what Simonides said (331e3–4). Yet, although Polemarchus rises to his father's defense and claims to be defending the view of justice he has just inherited from his father (331d4–8), the first thing we must note is that the saying he attributes to Simonides is not identical to the definition of justice Socrates attributed to Cephalus. The most obvious difference is that giving to each what is owed, the view of justice Polemarchus attributes to Simonides, leaves out part of telling the truth and returning what one has taken: it leaves out telling the truth. But if giving to each what is owed leaves out this half of the earlier definition, it also, if less obviously, broadens the other half, returning what one has taken. Giving to each what is owed, at least in its most ordinary and conventional meaning, provides a more general statement of the principle, or rule, which is expressed in a more limited way (or with reference to more specific instances) by returning what one has taken. This principle could be expressed still more generally: justice consists of respecting what belongs to each, and that means, especially, respecting private property. What belongs to us, in the sense of what is legally ours, is the most common meaning of what we are owed.

Now, insofar as Polemarchus understands Simonides' saying in this conventional way—which is the only way in which it would sup-

---

9. See Leo Strauss, "The Origins of Political Science and the Problem of Socrates: Six Public Lectures" *Interpretation* 23 (1996): 127–207, pp. 182–183; see also Mary Nichols, *Socrates and the Political Community* (Albany: State University of New York Press, 1987), p. 38; Sallis, pp. 322–323.

port Cephalus' view of justice—Socrates' earlier objection to Cephalus would still seem to hold. Polemarchus' appeal to the authority of Simonides does nothing to change the fact that one ought not to return weapons to a mad friend; and the replacement of "what one has taken" by the more general "what is owed" would seem only to bring out with greater breadth the implications of Socrates' objection. Yet rather than criticizing Polemarchus for not understanding that objection, or trying directly to refute the statement Polemarchus attributes to Simonides, a "wise and divine man," Socrates claims not to understand what Simonides meant (331e5–8). "For clearly," Socrates says, Simonides could not have meant what he and Cephalus were just talking about, "returning to anyone whatsoever something he has deposited when, of unsound mind, he demands it back" (331e8–332a1). Socrates presents this statement as a recapitulation of the earlier example, but in fact it is an expansion. Where, in the earlier example, the depositor was a friend, now it is "anyone whatsoever"; where the deposit was weapons, now it is just "something"; and where the one demanding the return was in a fit of rage, now he is only "of unsound mind."

This expansion reflects a point mentioned earlier, namely, that there are far-reaching implications to the admission that the rule (either returning what one has taken or, more generally, giving to each what is legally owed) should at times give way to our insistence that justice be good rather than harmful. If justice is to be something that does not cause harm, not only weapons—which can cause only more obvious harm—but *all* private property ought, in principle, to be contingent not merely on the sanity of the owner but on the capacity of the owner to put it to good or beneficial use. (Otherwise, justice would be that which requires the distribution of things in a way that is not advantageous; it would, in that sense, be harmful.) And since knowledge of who is fit to have what thus proves to be what is most needed to determine who should have what, such knowledge, and not laws, which are inevitably too crude and general, is the ideal determiner of justice.[10]

----

10. See Benardete, p. 15; see also Averroes, *Averroes on Plato's Republic*, trans. by Ralph Lerner (Ithaca: Cornell University Press), p. 7. For the most complete discussions of this point, and for further reflections to which I am indebted in this paragraph as well as more broadly in this chapter, see Strauss, "The Origins of Political

Following this line of thought, we begin to wonder whether our admission of exceptions to giving to each what is owed, in the sense of what is legally theirs—an admission necessary to preserve the goodness of justice—does not ultimately point to the abandonment of giving to each what is owed in favor of giving to each what is fitting, in the sense of what is good for them. That way justice could be expressed by a rule, giving to each what is fitting, that would seem never to be in conflict with justice being good. Socrates points to this movement from, in short, "owed" to "fitting" when, after again bringing to light the unacceptability of returning regardless of circumstances what has been deposited, he says, "and yet what has been deposited is, I suppose (or, 'surely': *pou*), owed" (332a1–2). In other words, the movement that is demanded away from the rule of giving to each what belongs to them (in the conventional or legal sense)[11] can be seen as a movement away from justice as giving to each what is owed. As Socrates strikingly puts it, once we recognize the superiority of giving to each what is fitting, it is "a riddle after the fashion of the poets" to retain the term "owed" (332b9–c3). Thus, from the problem raised about returning deposits, we seem to have been led very quickly beyond private property, beyond the laws that sanction private property, to the conclusion that it is better, and therefore more just, to give to each what is fitting, in the sense of what is good for them, than it is to give them what is owed, in the sense of what belongs to them.

Now, Socrates may encourage us to entertain this radical conclusion. But simply to accept it at this point would be too hasty. For one thing, the conversation does not turn immediately from "owed," in the conventional sense of what legally belongs to each, to "fitting,"

Science and the Problem of Socrates," p. 184, *The City and Man*, pp. 68–69, *Natural Right and History* (Chicago: University of Chicago Press, 1953), pp. 146–148.

11. I add the qualification "in the conventional or legal sense" because another way of formulating the issue at hand would be to ask whether something that supposedly (or legally) belongs to someone truly belongs to that person if it is not useful or good for him, since we mean by possessions something beneficial. See, for instance, the argument in the first chapter of Xenophon's *Oeconomicus*, especially the seventh section: in response to Socrates' statement of the view that a man's household is whatever he possesses, Critoboulos says, " 'Yes, by Zeus, . . . at least if what he possesses is good; for whatever is bad, by Zeus, I do not call a possession.' "

in the sense of what is good for each. Rather, the conversation turns to another, specific understanding of what it means to give to each what is fitting that is put forth, not by Socrates, but by Polemarchus, who certainly has in mind by this something other than giving to each what is good for them. Indeed, Polemarchus says that it is fitting to give enemies some *harm*, that is to say, the opposite of what is good for them (332b6–8).[12] Polemarchus understands "fitting" in this way: one gives what is fitting by helping friends and harming enemies. We might be tempted to say that in a different way he too moves from owed to fitting insofar as helping friends and harming enemies is a principle that he admits should override respect for private property or what is owed in the legal sense (332a9–b8). But Polemarchus does not present helping friends and harming enemies as a departure from what is owed, but rather as a clarification, or an interpretation, of the saying he attributed to Simonides that it is just to give to each what is owed. What Simonides meant, according to Polemarchus' expanded (or revised?) account, is that it is precisely by helping friends and harming enemies that one gives what is owed (332a9ff.). And by so giving what is owed, according to Polemarchus, one also gives what is fitting. Since our friends deserve our help, helping them is both owed and fitting, and since our enemies deserve to be harmed, harming them is also both owed and fitting. In other words, all three principles, helping friends and harming enemies, giving to each what is owed, and giving to each what is fitting, are united for Polemarchus.

In keeping with this understanding, Socrates uses both terms, owed and fitting, when he begins to question Polemarchus, or rather Polemarchus' Simonides, about justice understood as helping friends and harming enemies (see 332c5–8, 11–12). But remaining in the background throughout Socrates' critique of helping friends and harming enemies is the alternative understanding by which giving to each what is fitting means giving to each what is good for them, an understanding to which no notion of owing seems to belong (see again, 332b9–c3).

---

12. See Sallis, p. 330.

Socrates' Three-Part Critique of Justice as Helping Friends and Harming Enemies (332c5–336a10)

After bringing out Polemarchus' interpretation of Simonides to the effect that it is owed and fitting to help friends and harm enemies, Socrates puts a series of questions to Polemarchus' Simonides. Actually, Socrates begins not by asking a question in his own name but by posing to Polemarchus the hypothetical situation in which an anonymous "someone" might ask Simonides, "'Simonides, the art that gives what, that is owed and fitting, to what, is called medicine?'" (332c5–8). Polemarchus answers for Simonides, "the one that gives drugs, food, and drink to bodies" (332c9–10). Following along the same lines, Polemarchus responds to the next question, which asks about the art called cooking, by saying that it is the art that gives seasonings to meats (332c11–d1).[13] Socrates then uses this pattern to get Polemarchus (they cease for the time being to refer to Simonides) to state his opinion that justice is the art that gives benefits to friends and harms to enemies, and thus that the definition of justice is helping friends and harming enemies (332d2–9). Now, this procedure, which appears to have the purpose of getting a definition

---

13. Although medicine and cooking are said here to treat bodies and meats respectively, it might be more accurate to say that they treat patients and feasters. Viewed in this way, and taking into account that they both involve things that are eaten or otherwise ingested, the juxtaposition of these two examples raises a question about helping friends and harming enemies. Does one help one's friends by giving them what is good for them, even if they might not want it (like a doctor giving a patient bitter drugs), or by giving them merely what they want (like a cook catering to the tastes of his feasters) (Cf. Plato's *Gorgias* 464b2–466a3)? It is most likely the case that we (and Polemarchus) think that it is very easy to help our friends, since we understand this to be giving them what they want. But any true friend would grant that it is better to give his friends what is good for them, even if they do not want it. So the juxtaposition of these examples, like the coming discussion, serves to point out that helping friends is more difficult, and requires more knowledge, than we might think.

The juxtaposition of these two examples may raise another question as well. It is more plausible to say that the well-being of bodies is the end medicine than it is to say that the well-being of meats is the end of cooking; meats are clearly used as a mere means in cooking. Which, then, is the better analogy for the art of justice as helping friends and harming enemies? Are friends and enemies, their benefit and harm, the true or most final end of justice so understood?

of justice from Polemarchus, is strange, since at this point it already seems clear from what has come before that Polemarchus thinks justice is helping friends and harming enemies. It is true that he had spoken only of what is just (*dikaion*) and had not given a definition of justice (*dikaiosunē*). But if a formal definition of justice was all that was needed, it could easily have been gotten without these examples from the arts, merely by asking him, "So, Polemarchus, you think justice is helping friends and harming enemies?"[14] Why, then, this strange turn to the arts?

Apart from saying that the arts possess the flexibility and precision that comes from not being constrained by law—the flexibility and precision that the weapons example and its follow-ups suggested justice ought to have—perhaps we should not try to answer this question just yet, for the coming discussion raises it all the more. Indeed, this brief turn to the arts to define justice is only the prelude to a much longer examination of, or search for, the "art" of justice.

This search for the "art" of justice is, in turn, only the first part of a three-part critique of the definition of justice as helping friends and harming enemies. The three parts of this critique, the first including a kind of appendix (333e3–334b6) and the third a conclusion to the whole critique (335e1–336a10), are marked off by four exchanges that directly address the definition, respectively stating it, restating it, amending it, and finally rejecting it (332d7–8, 334b3–9, 335a6–11, 335e1–336a10). The three parts of the critique ask three questions: (1) In what respect is justice useful for helping friends and harming enemies? (2) Who are friends? and (3) Does it really belong to the just man to harm anyone whatsoever?

Part One (332d10–334b9)

In keeping with the prelude we have already seen, the first part of Socrates' critique of justice as helping friends and harming enemies proceeds by insisting that justice be viewed as an art. After leading Polemarchus to say that justice is the art that gives help to friends and harm to enemies, Socrates raises the following problem with justice

---

14. See Cross and Woozely, pp. 4–6.

so understood. The help and harm that justice, according to the definition, is supposed to give to friends and enemies (respectively) would seem always to be in the form of providing a particular good or service (or harm or disservice in the case of enemies) that is appropriate to a particular situation. But in each particular situation there is an expert, or specialist, who is better able than the just man to provide the appropriate help or harm.

Socrates begins with the examples of sickness and sailing. In the matter of sickness and health, the person most able to help friends who are sick and to harm enemies is the doctor, and with respect to the danger of the sea, the person most able to help friends who are sailing and to harm enemies is the pilot (332d10–e2). In what affair (*praxei*), or with respect to what work (*ergon*), then, is the just man the one most able to help friends and harm enemies (332e3–4)? It would seem to be impossible to locate a particular affair or work in which there would not be a particular expert better equipped by his knowledge to help friends and harm enemies than the just man.

Socrates does not, however, use this consideration to contest Polemarchus' reply that it is in making war and being an ally in battle that the just man is the one most able to help friends and harm enemies (332e5). Rather than asking, as he could have, whether the expert soldier is not better at making war and is not a more capable ally in battle than the just man (cf. 333d6–8), Socrates lets Polemarchus' answer stand as far as it goes and asks, instead, whether this does not mean that justice is useless in times of peace. For just as the doctor is useless for those who are not sick and the pilot is useless for those who are not sailing, so the just man would seem to be useless for those who are not at war (332e6–11). In keeping with the model of the arts, the "art" of justice would be limited in the same way the other arts are limited—that is, limited to the particular situation in which the particular art is needed.

Polemarchus is unwilling, of course, to accept the conclusion that justice is useless except in war, and he insists that it is useful also in peacetime (332e11–333a1). But in trying to maintain this position Polemarchus runs into the same problem that Socrates raised before and which he now pushes more rigorously. In any particular peacetime situation there is a particular expert, with a particular art, who is better able to help friends and harm enemies than the just man. So whereas it is easy to see that the farmer is useful in peacetime (for the acquisition of fruits) and that the shoemaker is as well (for the acquisition of shoes) it is more difficult to see where justice can fit in (333a2–9). Socrates asks Polemarchus, addressing him directly (Simonides continues to be left out), "for the use or acquisition of what would you claim justice to be useful in peacetime?" (333a10–11).[15]

Polemarchus comes up with "contracts" (333a12), and he then agrees with Socrates that by "contracts" (*sumbolaia*) he means "partnerships" (*koinōnēmata*) (333a13–14). *Koinōnēmata* (from *koinos*, "common") is the more general term, referring to common undertakings generally, including but not limited to those having to do with money (which would be the primary meaning of *sumbolaia*).[16] Yet, although Polemarchus accepts this expansion from *sumbolaia* to *koinōnēmata*, or from contracts to partnerships, he quickly retreats insofar as he identifies those partnerships in which the just man is a better partner than others as those partnerships having to do with money (333b10). He is forced to retreat by Socrates' reminders that in playing draughts the expert draughts player is a better partner than the just man, that in setting down bricks and stones the housebuilder is a better partner than the just man, and that in making musical notes the harpist is preferable (333b1–9).

But even Polemarchus' answer that the just man is a better partner than the others in money matters runs into difficulty. For if money is to be used, for instance, to buy or sell a horse or a ship, wouldn't it be better to have an expert, a horseman or a pilot, as your partner (333b11–c6)? It seems to be only when money (or anything

---

15. Contrary to the status accorded these arts today, there seems to be an ascent in Socrates' examples from those arts that are required for getting out of difficulties (medicine and piloting) to those arts by which good things are acquired in peacetime (farming and shoemaking). Here at 333a10–11, Socrates asks not only about acquisition (*ktēsin*) but about use (*chreian*) as well; the use of good things in peacetime may be even a further step up. In this connection, it may be noteworthy that the next examples are draughts-playing and housebuilding, possible stand-ins for dialectics and lawgiving, rivals, perhaps, for the title of the most architectonic art. See Allan Bloom, *The Republic of Plato* (New York: Basic Books, 1968), note 24 to the translation.

16. See Bloom's note 23; see also James Adam's commentary, *The Republic of Plato* (Cambridge: Cambridge University Press, 1965), p. 16.

for that matter)[17] is not being used, but only being guarded, that justice is useful (333c5–d11). Socrates' argument, by calling attention to the superiority of a particular expert in every conceivable situation, runs justice so far into the ground that he gets Polemarchus reluctantly to agree that for any given thing, justice is useless in the thing's use and useful only in its uselessness. And, needless to say, by this conclusion justice is "not something very serious" (333e1–2).

But Socrates goes even further. Adding insult to injury, he uses the identification of justice with guarding to argue that the just man must be a clever thief and that justice must be a certain art of *stealing* (333e2–b6)! In an appendix to the attempt to locate the usefulness of justice (consider *tode de skepsōmetha*, 333e3) Socrates finally allows justice to be an art, if an art that is not very serious, but only to argue that justice, like all the other arts, must then be a certain expertise that can be used for either helping or harming, or, as we would say, for good or evil. The man who is cleverest at punching is also the one cleverest at guarding against punches; the man who is clever at guarding against disease is also the one cleverest at producing disease; and the man who is good at guarding an army is also the one good at stealing the enemy's plans (333e2–334a3). Deviating from his previous approach, Socrates does not use this line of argument, as he might have, to show that the just man cannot be even the best guard because there are experts at guarding against each particular danger. Rather, by allowing, and by playing upon, the claim that the just man is clever at guarding (at least money), Socrates argues that since "of whatever someone is a clever guard, of this he is also a clever thief" (334a5), the just man, as a clever guard, must then be a clever thief (334a7–8). According to the conclusion Socrates now attributes to Polemarchus, Homer, and Simonides (Socrates resurrects Simonides at this incriminating moment), justice is a certain art of stealing, albeit for the benefit of friends and the harm of enemies (334b3–6).

Polemarchus objects, of course, to this conclusion (334b7). And he is right to object. For while there is a certain justification for

---

17. By mentioning a sickle, a shield, and a lyre (and then "all other things") Socrates restores at 333d3–11 something of the more general range of *koinōnē-mata*—but only to set up, or broaden, his further attack.

Socrates' argument in the fact that the definition of justice as helping friends and harming enemies says nothing explicitly to restrict the means by which one is to help friends and harm enemies (and therefore would seem to permit stealing),[18] Socrates has been misconstruing Polemarchus' replies, and accordingly the character of justice as Polemarchus understands it, throughout this whole argument. The outrageousness of the conclusion reached by the last exchange, or what I have called the appendix, makes only more manifest the problem of the whole argument. The conclusion of the appendix, again, is that justice, as an art of guarding, is also an art of stealing. This is so since arts provide only the expertise and not what we might call the just intention; they can be used, we would say, justly or unjustly. But doesn't our very characterization of the arts in this way reveal the problem of making justice an art of guarding and, indeed, the problem of the whole argument that uses the arts as a model for justice? By saying that the arts can be used justly or unjustly, that they are, as we would say, morally neutral, don't we reveal that what we mean by justice is something essentially different from art? When Polemarchus said that justice is useful in war and in contracts (or partnerships) he surely did not mean that the just man is as such a knowledgeable and skillful ally in battle or a knowledgeable and skillful partner in peaceful ventures. He meant that the just man is good to have on your side because he is *loyal* and *trustworthy*. By pressing the model of the arts, Socrates disregards the importance of the *just intention* (as the appendix makes only more clear than it already was). Yet what is the just intention but what Polemarchus, and indeed all of us, mean, perhaps most of all, by justice? In other words, in the attempt to locate justice as an art—an attempt which ends up leading to the conclusion that justice is virtually nothing, and that what little it is can, absurdly, be used justly or unjustly—Socrates

---

18. Polemarchus' objection to the present conclusion reflects his understanding that helping friends and harming enemies, in its barest sense, is not all there is to justice. The least that would have to be added is that justice is helping friends and harming enemies only by certain means. By objecting to stealing, moreover, Polemarchus shows some continued or renewed concern for the original sense of "owed," that is, for the sanctity of private property. Cf. Dobbs, "The Piety of Thought," pp. 675–676; Julia Annas, *An Introduction to Plato's Republic* (Oxford: Clarendon Press, 1981), pp. 28–29.

abstracts from the beginning from justice, at least from what we commonly take to be the heart of justice, the just intention.[19]

But why, then, does Socrates travel down this path? Why does he focus on the knowledge or expertise found in the arts to the neglect of the just intention that belongs to, or even *is*, justice? Perhaps he does so to provoke this very question, and to encourage us to reflect in turn on the relationship between knowledge or expertise and the just intention, or to encourage us to question the just intention in light of the question of knowledge or expertise. That the just intention is at least in some respect questionable can be seen in an immediate way by considering that although the knowledge of the arts is not sufficient by itself to help friends and harm enemies, neither is the just intention sufficient by itself. Socrates' argument repeatedly points out that experts, as experts, are more *able* to help friends and harm enemies than the just man, as a just man (see again, e.g., 332d10–11). We can now respond, as Polemarchus should have, that the greater *ability* of the experts to help friends and harm enemies does not yet ensure their *willingness* to do so; only the just intention would seem to ensure that. But while this seems to redeem the importance of the just intention, the fact remains that by itself, without the knowledge of how to help or harm, the willingness or intention to help or harm is itself deficient and lacks the usefulness we also expect from justice. A man of good intentions who wants more than anything to help but whose bumbling attempts bring nothing but harm, while he might be forgiven and even praised for his efforts, cannot be fully respected or admired; such a man fails to accomplish the very things his intention seeks to accomplish, and in this respect he falls short of his own standards.[20]

---

19. Consider Aristotle, *Nicomachean Ethics* 1129a7–16; compare Kant, *Groundwork*, pp. 61–65, 82–84. See also Richard Lewis Nettleship, *Lectures on the Republic of Plato* (London: Macmillan and Company, 1925), p. 22; Reeve, p. 8; Cross and Woozely, pp. 11–15; Nichols, pp. 44–45; Dobbs, "The Piety of Thought," p. 675; Sallis, p. 333.

20. See Xenophon, *Memorabilia* I.2.50–55. As I mentioned in my introduction, the absolute value of the good will "in itself," that is, apart from any consequences, is one of the pillars of ordinary moral consciousness in Kant's presentation. Kant claims: "Even if, by some special disfavour of destiny or by the niggardly endowment of step-motherly nature, this will is entirely lacking in power to carry out its intentions; if by its utmost effort it still accomplishes nothing, and only good will is

Still, this means no more than that the just intention must be coupled with knowledge if it is to serve the ends it wants to serve, that the just intention needs the knowledge of the arts as the means of doing what it disposes the just man to do. We can, however, wonder about the relation of the just intention to another sort of knowledge different from that possessed by the experts in the arts: knowledge of what is good for people. Socrates' argument implicitly points to this kind of knowledge insofar as it too—indeed it most of all—is needed to help friends and harm enemies; it is needed to guide the arts, to know when and to whom they should be applied.[21] Yet while we can see that the knowledge of the arts is needed to serve the just intention, and that knowledge of what is good for people is as well, at least in the case of this latter kind of knowledge we can turn the question around. With knowledge of what is good for people, why would the just intention be needed? We can put this question in terms of partnerships (koinōnēmata), since Socrates himself raises that consideration and Polemarchus readily goes along with it (333a13–14). Why, or in what case, would knowledge of what is good for people not be enough to guarantee commitment to a partnership? For if a partnership is good for all of the partners, then it would seem that the

---

left (not, admittedly, as a mere wish, but as the straining of every means so far as they are in our control); even then it would shine like a jewel for its own sake as something which has its full value in itself. Its usefulness or fruitlessness can neither add to, nor subtract from, this value" (Groundwork, p. 62). Socrates' argument in this section, however, forces us to question this claim. Don't we share Polemarchus' dissatisfaction with the thought of the just man as useless? And indeed, doesn't it belong to the good intention itself to be concerned not just with its own purity but with its effects? Kant himself, after all, acknowledges and even stresses that it makes a great difference to the moral man that his actions not be mere noble yet futile efforts, but that they actually contribute to the betterment of the world, that they be at least small steps toward bringing about "general happiness" (see, e.g., Critique of Pure Reason, A809–813/B837–841).

21. See Bloom, "Interpretive Essay" in The Republic of Plato, p. 322: "The doctor can produce health, but that health is good he does not learn from medicine, and similarly with all the other arts. They deal with partial goods which presuppose a knowledge of the whole good to which they minister. . . . To help a sick friend one needs not only a doctor but someone who knows to whom health is fitting and how many other goods should be sacrificed to it, and who can direct the doctor to do what will most help the patient." Compare Plato's Gorgias 511e6–512b2; Averroes, pp. 86–88; Annas, An Introduction, p. 26.

partners would need to possess only knowledge of what is good for them; there would be no need, in principle, for the just intention. Taking into account that we have at least some self-concern, knowledge of what is good for people, which of course includes knowledge of what is good for oneself, would seem to be enough to ensure our commitment to anything that is good for us.

Don't we have to conclude, then, that the just intention is truly needed only in circumstances, or partnerships, that are not good for everyone involved? That is to say, isn't the just intention truly needed only in partnerships that are flawed or defective from the point of view of the good, that is, ones that require a contribution from at least some members that is bad for them? This conclusion, which I think we must draw, can be expressed in terms of the common good, a consideration clearly raised by the mention of partnerships (*koinōnēmata*): justice as *devotion* to the common good is needed, in principle, only when there is no true common good in the strict sense.

Now, it may be needless to say that this seems to be a disturbing fact about justice, that the just intention or devotion to the common good or to others—what we mean perhaps most of all by justice—is truly needed only in defective circumstances or arrangements. But I also wonder whether this seemingly disturbing fact does not also bring out what we regard as so admirable about justice. For isn't the very doing of things that are not good for oneself, but serve the higher common good, the most impressive aspect of justice? Polemarchus, we recall, pointed to making war and being an ally in battle as the work of the just man (332e5). And wouldn't he find it most impressive if that called for risking one's own life for the sake of another, or for the sake of the city? The very flaw, in other words, in the common good strictly understood (i.e., as good for *all*) would seem to be necessary to make possible sacrifice for the sake of the common good understood as something distinct from and beyond the good of the individual.[22]

To this, however, I want to add a final reflection, or ask a final set of questions. We have just seen that it is the very fact that the com-

---

22. Compare Aristotle, *Nicomachean Ethics* 1129b25–1130a8. Consider also Kant, *Critique of Practical Reason*, pp. 86–87, and David Hume, *Enquiries Concerning Human Understanding and Concerning the Principles of Morals*, 3rd ed. (Oxford: Clarendon Press, 1975), pp. 183–192.

mon good strictly understood can be flawed that makes possible self-sacrifice for the sake of something higher than one's (mere) self. Yet don't we also think—as our enthusiasm about that point suggests we do—that such sacrifice is also somehow the greatest good for the individual himself, the very one who, we think, sacrifices? By sacrificing oneself for the sake of justice, doesn't one elevate oneself and thereby gain the greatest or most essential good not of the body but of what is higher, the soul? But if that is true, then it is hard to see how we can still speak of sacrifice. In some sense, we might be able to if, while the one who "sacrifices" does in fact get the greatest good for himself, he does not act for that reason—in other words, if he secures his own good without acting for the sake of his own good. For that to be the case, though, one's own good would have to be a genuinely subordinate concern, and at least the strength and importance of our belief that sacrifice is ultimately good for us—our experience of it as promising a surpassing happiness, a happiness of which we believe it makes us deserving—suggests that our concern for our own good may never play this subordinate role. And if our own good is always our fundamental concern, if even our "sacrifices" are done for the sake of our own good, the pride of place that we might want to attribute to the just intention—to the resolve always to do the just thing whether it is good for us or not—would seem properly to belong instead to knowledge of what is good for people, and in particular to knowledge of what is good for oneself.

The crucial question, though, of whether we ever act for the sake of something other than our own good—or more precisely what we take to be our own good (since we make mistakes)—is at most indirectly pointed to merely as a question by Socrates' line of argument. It is not answered, nor is the reflection I have just outlined meant to settle the issue, but only to articulate its significance. By trying to do even this, however, I may have strayed too far from the conversation at hand. Let us hasten back, then, to the critique of justice as helping friends and harming enemies.

Part Two (334c1–335b1)

In the second part of his critique of justice as helping friends and harming enemies, Socrates raises the problem not of knowing how to help friends and harm enemies but of knowing who one's friends and enemies whom it is just to help and harm are in the first place. Socrates points out to Polemarchus that although it seems easy to know who one's friends are—those who seem good—sometimes people misjudge such that they take as their friends those who are not truly good; and they do the same with enemies: they misjudge such that they hate, or take as their enemies, those who merely seem to them to be bad, but are in fact good (334c1–8). The problem from the standpoint of justice is that in those cases in which people misjudge, if it is nonetheless just to help friends and harm enemies, it would be just to help the bad and harm the good (334c10–d1). Given the option by Socrates, "Do you say friends are those who seem to each to be good, or those who are truly good even if they don't seem to be, and likewise with enemies?" (334c1–3), Polemarchus originally goes with the commonsensical choice that belief or opinion is the basis of friendship and enmity. But this has the result—the one he proves to be unable to stomach—that by this view of friendship and enmity, coupled with his view that justice is helping friends and harming enemies, it could be just for the good man, who he agrees is just and not the sort to do injustice, to harm those who have done nothing unjust (334d3–6).

Faced with this result, Polemarchus gladly accepts Socrates' next proposal, namely, that it is just to help the just and harm the unjust, as an amendment that strikes him as "finer" than what was said before (334d9–11). When Socrates points out, however, that this amendment takes them so far from justice as helping friends and harming enemies that, under the new view, it would be just for all those who misjudge the character of their friends and enemies to *harm friends* and *help enemies*,[23] Polemarchus decides that he had better salvage his (or Simonides') definition of justice by going back and changing the definition of friends and enemies (334d12–e6).

---

23. I am following Adam (p. 19) in reading *ponēroi gar autois eisin* at 334e2 as "for their friends are bad" against D. J. Allen (*Plato: Republic I* [Bristol: Bristol Classical Press, 1993], p. 90) and Godofredus Stallbaum (*Platonis Opera Omnia*, ed. by Leonardo Taran [New York: Garland Publishing, 1980], Volume 3, Part 1, p. 49), who suggest reading *autois* as an ethic rather than a possessive dative: "for their friends are bad in their eyes." As Adam points out, this latter reading is inconsistent with the view expressed at 334c1–5, a view that is not revised until after 334e2.

What "they" had previously set down as the definition of a friend, the one who seems good, should be changed, Polemarchus says, to the one who seems good and in fact is good; and the parallel change should be made with respect to enemies (334e8–335a2). Socrates then restates this new view for Polemarchus as if he were just checking to make sure that he and Polemarchus are on the same page: "According to this argument, then, it seems that the good man will be a friend, and the bad man an enemy" (335a3–4). Now, although Polemarchus readily agrees with Socrates' restatement and seems to regard it as identical to what he had said, we should note that it is not precisely, or merely, a restatement. It extends and makes even more radical the departure from everyday friendship and enmity that is implicit in Polemarchus' new definition of friends and enemies (compare 334c4–5, 334e10–335a2, and 335a3–4). Whereas Polemarchus had said that the friend or enemy is the one who *seems* good or bad (respectively) *and is* good or bad, making seeming and being the *two* requirements, Socrates' formulation says nothing about seeming good or bad—the only requirement is being good or bad. This change, which implies that the categories of friends and enemies could simply be replaced by the categories of those who are good and bad,[24] does seem, however, to be warranted by the logic of the argument in which Polemarchus himself has come to demand that actual goodness and badness carry the day over apparent goodness and badness. If left at Polemarchus' new definition of friends and enemies, without Socrates' amendatory restatement, the argument would not do justice to those who are good without seeming to be, or to those who are bad without seeming to be (cf. 334c1–3).

So, by following out the demand that the just man not harm others who are good or just,[25] Socrates and Polemarchus seem to have arrived, just before Socrates' final summary of this part of their con-

---

24. To take the case of friends (the parallel holds true of enemies), if goodness is the sole and sufficient criterion for being a friend—that is, if everyone who is good is thereby a friend and there are no friends who are not good—then "friend" is not needed, and indeed it cannot exist, as a category of its own separate from "good." Cf. Adam, p. 20.

25. Socrates' argument also appeals, although not as crucially, to the demand that the just man not help those who are bad or unjust (compare 334d3–8 with what precedes and follows).

versation, at the view that justice is helping the good (who are *ipso facto* friends) and harming the bad (who are *ipso facto* enemies). But what would this view mean if we tried to put it into action?

It would mean, to begin with, that all supposed friendships (to say nothing yet about enemies) would have to be revised in light of the sole consideration of whether each friend is good. The reasons we are attached to those we ordinarily take to be our friends other than that they are good—for instance, that they are similar to us, or that they are *our* friends—would have to be regarded as prejudices that serve only to cloud our judgment. In addition to this, and on a larger scale, the view that justice is helping the good and harming the bad would also mean, if it were to be put into practice, that all existing political divisions would have to be replaced by the cosmopolitan alliance of those who are good. If the definition of justice as helping friends and harming enemies, as Polemarchus originally intended it, is the consummate political understanding of justice, which sees the world as divided into various groups, or cities, all potentially in conflict with one's own group or city (see 332e5), Socrates has led Polemarchus to a new definition of justice that is apolitical to an extreme.[26] Considering the almost certainly inevitable division of the world into multiple political bodies whose interests are not always in perfect harmony, Socrates has pushed Polemarchus to an understanding of justice that no city, and no individual who must be a member of a city, could reasonably act on. Although the definition of justice as helping friends and harming enemies, as Polemarchus originally intended it, allows, or even requires, the harming of just men,[27]

---

26. Cf. Benardete, pp. 16–17. In this section and other instances, I will speak of "cities" rather than countries or nations. The city (*polis*) was, of course, the basic unit of political life in ancient Greece.

27. Even by its own logic, the definition of justice as helping friends and harming enemies makes at least some just acts inseparable from harming just men. Consider a war between two cities. When a soldier harms one of his enemies and thereby helps his friends, he harms someone whom the definition would label a just man, since presumably his enemy is helping his own side and thereby helping his own friends and harming his own enemies. It could be said, in response to this, that the definition does not object to the harming of just men but only to the harming of friends. Yet, even if the definition itself does not regard the harming of just men as

it is impossible to do away entirely with that understanding of justice without becoming a sitting duck.

But why, then, does Socrates push for a view of justice that would be impossible, or at least extremely foolish, to live by? Surely he is not naive about the obstacles involved. Even in the just city he will construct in speech later in the *Republic*, a city that breaks the bounds of the possible in many respects (see 540e5–541a7 for the clearest example), Socrates does not try to do away with the necessity that it be a particular city willing to be hostile toward other cities.[28] Indeed, he is even criticized by Aristotle for having gone too far in the direction opposite to the one in which he leads Polemarchus here (see *Politics* 1327b38–1328a16).

Socrates cannot mean, then, for this radical understanding of justice, that it is just to help the good (whoever and wherever they are) and to harm the bad (whoever and wherever they are), to be actually practicable; but by leading Polemarchus down this unreasonable path, Socrates does bring to light one of the ways in which political life inevitably sacrifices some of the apparent demands of justice. The demand we make, and Polemarchus makes (334d5–8), that everyone get their due, has to be sacrificed in the face of the overwhelming fact that political reality forbids us to try such a thing. Indeed, as much as we think that justice demands giving to each their due, or what they deserve, so we also think that justice cannot destroy the city, that it must be politically feasible.[29] Yet, although this means that there is an excuse or warrant for not always giving to each what they deserve, it remains true that when political life requires that not everyone be given what they deserve it fails to live up to everything we want and hope for from justice.

---

unjust, those like Polemarchus who are the proponents of the definition do, and they may even want to transform the definition for that reason (see again 334d9–e6).

28. Consider, e.g., the discussion of the noble guard dogs at 375a2ff.; the first part of the noble lie at 414b1–e6; and the discussion of the city's foreign policy at 466e4ff. See Strauss, *The City and Man*, p. 73; Leon Craig, *The War Lover* (Toronto: University of Toronto Press, 1994), pp. 3–21; Sallis, p. 333. Consider also that it was Socrates, not Polemarchus, who first raised the question of enemies at 332b5.

29. Compare Aristotle, *Politics* 1281a11–38.

In light of this problem, that we both believe in the rightfulness and recognize the impracticality of the most extreme demands of justice, it is worth noting that when Socrates offers his final summary of this part of the conversation he does not stick strictly to the conclusion he and Polemarchus had reached. We recall that he had led Polemarchus to the extreme view that the good are *ipso facto* friends and the bad are *ipso facto* enemies and that the implication of this was that justice as helping friends and harming enemies should mean, and so could even be replaced by, justice as helping the good and harming the bad.[30] Yet, when he offers his final summary of the change required in Polemarchus' (or Simonides') definition of justice, Socrates says this: "You [Polemarchus] order us, then, to amend the just as we first spoke of it in saying that it is just to help the friend and harm the enemy; for now we are to say, in addition to this, that it is just to help the friend, if he is good, and to harm the enemy, if he is bad" (335a6–10). By referring to the *particular* cases in which the friend is good (*ton men philon agathon onta*) or the enemy is bad (*ton d' echthron kakon onta*), Socrates' summary implicitly allows for the possibility of the cases in which the friend is not good or the enemy is not bad. To this extent, the summary diverges from the conclusion of the argument it is ostensibly summarizing. For the argument left no place for friends who are not good or enemies who are not bad, since it declared that the good and friends are one and the same, and so with the bad and enemies (cf. 335a3–5). Socrates' supposed summary falls somewhere between the original understanding of justice as helping friends and harming enemies and the extreme revision that justice is helping the good and harming the bad. It leaves this quandary: it says, or at least it seems to imply, that one can have friends who are not good and enemies who are not bad, but it also implies that it would not be just to help such friends and harm such enemies. Perhaps we can sum up the results of this supposed summary by saying that it restores the ordinary understanding of who friends and enemies are, and that it removes the demand to help or harm those one does not know, but that it also leaves a harsh light on the questionable justice of helping friends who are not good and harming enemies who are not bad.

---

30. See note 24 above.

Part Three (335b2–335e6)

If Socrates finishes the second part of his critique of justice as helping friends and harming enemies by backing off from the extreme
argument of that part, he opens the third part with a question that is
even more extreme, or even more radical, than anything in the second part. He asks Polemarchus whether it belongs to a just man
(*estin . . . dikaiou*) to harm anyone whatsoever (335b2–3). Polemarchus responds, as almost anyone would, that it certainly does
belong to a just man to harm some people, namely those who are
bad and enemies, whom one ought to harm (335b4–5).[31] What
Polemarchus surely has in mind is that certain people deserve to be
harmed for their wickedness: the thief, for instance, deserves a beating as punishment for his thievery. Yet, while Polemarchus is in all
likelihood thinking about punishments that inflict pain on the
wicked as retribution for their wickedness, Socrates asks not about
the pain of such punishments but about whether they make the one
who suffers them better or worse. And by better or worse, Socrates
means better or worse with respect to the virtue of the particular kind
of being the sufferer is. He uses the analogies of horses and dogs.
Socrates leads Polemarchus to agree that horses, when they are
harmed, become not better but worse, and worse with respect to the
virtue not of dogs but of horses; and so with dogs, when they are
harmed, they become worse, and worse with respect to the virtue not
of horses but of dogs (335b6–12). But there is something strange
about this line of argument. For is it true that when a horse, to take
that example, is harmed, it necessarily becomes a worse horse? If a
horse were whipped or kicked, for instance, it might have no effect on
the virtue of the horse, or it might even make the horse a better horse.
Doesn't the training of horses involve such beatings? Of course, in the
case in which the harming of the horse makes the horse a better horse,
one could then ask whether it is really a "harming." And this is
Polemarchus' dilemma: Socrates gives him only two choices, either
the horse becomes a better horse or it becomes a worse one, and

---

31. Notice that Polemarchus speaks at this point of those who are bad *and* enemies, apparently following Socrates' moderating summary from the preceding section rather than the more radical view by which there would be no need to use both
terms.

Polemarchus has to go with the latter alternative because if he were to go with the former the harming would no longer truly be a harming.[32]

Having thus forced the conclusion that horses and dogs become worse when they are harmed, Socrates applies his dubious argument to human beings. Human beings too, he gets Polemarchus to agree, become worse when they are harmed, and worse with respect to the virtue of human beings (335c1–3). But, Socrates next asks, isn't justice the virtue of human beings, or human virtue (335c4)? Polemarchus, although offered no argument for this all-important claim, would never deny it, given his love of justice, and so he agrees that this too is necessary (335c5).[33] Putting these two steps together, Socrates draws the conclusion that when human beings are harmed they necessarily become more unjust—and Polemarchus must reluctantly agree (335c6–8). According to this conclusion, any time a human being is harmed, for instance when he is beaten for deserting his side in battle or even when he is merely fined for cheating in his business dealings, he necessarily becomes more unjust.

It is on the basis of this questionable conclusion that Socrates then tries to show that a just man would not harm anyone. For if harming people makes them more unjust, his argument runs, a just man would have to make people more unjust if he were to harm them. But just as musicians cannot make men unmusical by music,

---

32. Compare the somewhat different interpretation that Bloom offers of this passage. According to Bloom, Socrates is suggesting that harm ought to be understood as consisting *only* in becoming worse in virtue ("Interpretive Essay," p. 325). This interpretation, it seems to me, rests on a misreading of 335b6 and following ("Do horses, when they are harmed, become better or worse? . . .") as simply equating being harmed and becoming worse, rather than understanding the latter as a result of the former. Bloom's reading would perhaps make Socrates' argument more logically sound, but only at the expense of making it even more extreme and incredible. Common sense would also rebel at the similar suggestion of Friedländer that "strictly speaking, we can harm or injure another person only if we deprive his soul of its intrinsic excellence (*oikeia aretē*) . . ." (*Plato*, Volume 2, p. 59).

33. On the thought that justice is human virtue and the basis of Polemarchus' agreement to this suggestion see Dobbs, "The Piety of Thought," pp. 678–679 and n. 19. Dobbs brings out the convictions and hopes that are implicit in Polemarchus' agreement; he thus shows that, even though Socrates makes no argument here, Annas is wrong to conclude that the present step in the dialogue is groundless (see Annas, *An Introduction*, pp. 32–33).

and horsemen cannot make men bad horsemen by horsemanship, so it would seem unacceptable to say that just men can make others unjust by their justice, or, in general (*sullēbdēn*), that good men can make others vicious by their virtue (335c9–d2). To these analogies from the arts, which are open to doubt since the arts *would* seem to make their possessors capable of damaging the skill of another (recall that the arts can be used for harm as well as benefit: 333e3–334a9), Socrates adds the analogies of heat and dryness. Just as cooling is not the work (*ergon*) of heat but of its opposite, and wetting is not the work of dryness but of its opposite, so harming is not the work of the good but of its opposite (335d3–7). And since, as Polemarchus agrees, the just man is good, that means that harming is not the work of the just man but of his opposite, the unjust man (335d9–12). This last line of argument that uses the analogies of heat and dryness differs slightly from the preceding one that spoke of the arts insofar as it rests less on the view that harming necessarily makes the harmed unjust than on the simpler view that justice, something good, cannot cause harm, something bad.

At any rate, Socrates succeeds in getting Polemarchus to agree that it is not the work of the just man to harm either a friend or anyone else (335d11–13), and, finally, that it is in no way just to harm anyone (335e5–6). But although Socrates convinces Polemarchus, we should not be so quick to offer our own assent. For in addition to the difficulties in Socrates' arguments that we have already indicated, we can raise at least the further problem that this conclusion, like the one we considered in the previous section (see pp. 43–44 above), would be impossible to live by. If just men refused to harm anyone, if only unjust men were willing to harm others, unjust men would have the run of the earth. Certainly some measure of harming on the part of just men is necessary, if for no other reason than to deter unjust men from committing continual unjust acts. Socrates and Polemarchus' conclusion, then, would have to be amended at least this much to take this ugly necessity into account: the just man does not want to harm anyone, but he will do so when—and only when—it is necessary in order to deter unjust men.[34]

---

34. See Plato, *Laws* 731b3–c1.

But there is something odd about even this conclusion. For in saying that the need to harm unjust men is an ugly necessity, that the just man would only reluctantly harm unjust men, haven't we forgotten that unjust men *deserve* the harm, or punishment, they get? Indeed, haven't we forgotten entirely about the retribution that just men may rightfully take against, that they even *owe*, unjust men? Where did such retribution go? It was dropped because it would require that just men make others more unjust (on the view that all harming makes the sufferer more unjust), or because it would make justice, something good, the cause of harm, something bad. But, as we wondered earlier, does all harming really make the sufferer more unjust? And, more important, don't unjust men deserve the harm (whatever its result for their virtue) that they receive at the hands of just men? Such harming may not be good in the sense of being good for the unjust men, but it would seem to be good in what we regard as the more important sense that unjust men do not deserve something good, but something bad, and it is just, and good, to give people what they deserve (consider 332b6–8; see also 334d9–11 and 335b4–5). From this perspective, it would seem that the analogies of the arts and of heat and dryness were inappropriate and misleading. For while the arts and heat and dryness may not be able to cause their opposites (although this is questionable in the case of the arts), the arts and heat and dryness are amoral, which justice, it is almost redundant to say, is not. Justice is a different sort of thing, and though we think that it is good, we nonetheless think also that it is able to cause something bad, at least in the sense of bad for those who deserve something bad. We might even say that this is part of its goodness.[35]

Deserved harm, or rightful punishment, then, is what Socrates' arguments in this section neglect most of all. Yet perhaps it is more accurate to say that Socrates' arguments do not so much neglect

---

35. See Kant, *Critique of Practical Reason*, p. 63: "When . . . someone who delights in annoying and vexing peace-loving folk receives at last a right good beating, it is certainly an ill, but everyone approves of it and considers it as good in itself even if nothing further should result from it; nay, even he who gets the beating must acknowledge, in his reason, that justice has been done to him, because he sees the proportion between welfare and well-doing, which reason inevitably holds before him, here put into practice."

deserved harm as provide a critique of the belief that unjust men deserve to be harmed. Polemarchus certainly began from that belief (335b4–5), and yet by the end of this section Socrates has secured at least his temporary agreement to a conclusion that replaces that belief with the view that harming is never just (335e5–6). However, if Socrates' arguments are meant to be a critique of the belief that unjust men deserve to be harmed, or punished, our earlier objections are enough, I think, to show that the critique is inadequate, at least in its explicit reasoning. Polemarchus should not have been convinced.[36]

Nevertheless, there may still be a way, if one that is less explicit, in which Socrates indicates in this section the beginnings of a more adequate critique of the belief that unjust men deserve to be harmed. In this regard, let us note and briefly consider the relation of a few points that Socrates' procedure serves to call to our attention. First, as we have seen, Socrates' procedure makes clear at the beginning that Polemarchus thinks, as almost all of us do, that unjust men deserve to suffer (335b2–5, 335c1–3). Socrates' procedure makes clear also, however, that Polemarchus thinks, as again almost all of us do, that justice is good for the just man. Polemarchus does not think that human beings who are harmed and thereby become more unjust are harmed less by becoming more unjust, but rather that becoming more unjust adds to, or is part of, the harm—implying that they would benefit by being made more just rather than more unjust, or, in short, that it is better to be just than unjust (335b6–d1). Indeed, Polemarchus agrees with what is perhaps the greatest claim that could be raised on behalf of justice: that it is human virtue (335c4–5; see also 335d9–10). Yet, one could then ask Polemarchus, or anyone

---

36. As for why Polemarchus was convinced, it seems to have been the final and simplest part of Socrates' argument that swayed him, namely that justice, as good, cannot be the cause of harm, that is, of bad or evil (compare Polemarchus' reply at 335d13 with his more reluctant acceptance of the first part of Socrates' argument at 335c8). To speculate about why this thought carries such power for Polemarchus, it is perhaps best to understand it in connection with his belief that justice is human virtue (335c4–5). It may be that Socrates speaks here to Polemarchus' deepest hope about justice, a hope to find in justice, as human virtue, a good that is in no way marred or tainted by evil; this hope, moreover, as a wish to be free of the necessity of evils, might lead one, if only for a moment, to overlook or "wish away" the harsher facts of the world, such as the existence of wickedness and thus the need for good men to cause harm. Cf. Nichols, pp. 43–48, especially p. 47.

else who holds the same opinions: If justice is good for the just man, why would anyone be unjust? Wouldn't it have to be because that person is somehow ignorant of the goodness of justice? No one, it would seem, would knowingly choose to be unjust if it is bad for him. But do the unjust deserve to suffer even more for having unknowingly (and thus in a sense involuntarily) chosen something through which they must, if justice is good and injustice bad, be suffering already?[37]

Polemarchus' agreement that it is in no way just to harm anyone, whether he should have agreed to that or not, completes Socrates' critique of justice as helping friends and harming enemies. For on the basis of that agreement Socrates gets Polemarchus to agree to this final rejection of justice as helping friends and harming enemies: "If, then, someone says that it is just to give to each what is owed, and he means by this that harm is owed to enemies by the just man, and help to friends, the one who said these things was not wise, for what he said is not true" (335e1–4). Of course, the "one" who said these things, the "someone" who interpreted giving to each what is owed to mean helping friends and harming enemies, was Polemarchus, who implicitly agrees here that he was not wise (335e6). All that can rightly be attributed to Simonides, Polemarchus' source, is the saying that it is just to give to each what is owed, not the interpretation that this means that it is just to help friends and harm enemies. Indeed, Socrates now gets Polemarchus, in an ironic turn for the one whose view of justice included, perhaps above all, helping friends in battle (see 332e5), to agree to be his ally in battle against "someone" who would attribute to Simonides or any other "wise and blessed man"

---

37. See Plato, *Laws* 731c1–d3, *Apology of Socrates* 25c5–26a7, and *Cleitophon* 407d2–e2 for more explicit and fuller statements of this argument. Consider also the following question, which could be asked about anyone who holds the view that Polemarchus does at least at the beginning of this section. Polemarchus believes, as I have just pointed out, that justice is good, but also that unjust men deserve to suffer. Yet does the belief that unjust men deserve to suffer, and the zeal to punish them, indicate a doubt of the first belief, that is, that justice is good? For if one were utterly convinced that the just are better off than the unjust, wouldn't one be content with, or even pity, the situation of unjust men who (one would be convinced) are suffering already by being unjust? Consider in this regard the later statement of Adeimantus at 366c4–6 that someone with sufficient knowledge that the just life is best would not feel anger toward the unjust.

the interpretation that giving to each what is owed means helping friends and harming enemies (335e7–10).

By rejecting only Polemarchus' particular interpretation of the saying that it is just to give to each what is owed, and by remarking that that interpretation does not live up to Simonides' wisdom and blessedness, Socrates seems to suggest that giving to each what is owed could still be the correct definition of justice, if it had a better interpretation. But what would that interpretation be? One possibility, although it would be "a riddle after the fashion of the poets" to use the term "owed" if this is what one meant (recall 332b9–c3), is that giving to each what is owed should mean giving to each what is fitting, in the sense of what is good for them. This possibility, which we considered earlier (see pp. 29–30 above) and which has in some sense been lurking in the background throughout Socrates' conversation with Polemarchus, would have the merit of responding to many of the difficulties Socrates has raised both in his critique of justice as helping friends and harming enemies and, before that, in his discussion of returning another's property. Giving to each what is fitting, since it would require knowledge of what it is fitting for each, could be accomplished only by the wise, who would have to be in a position to distribute all things according to the needs and abilities of each. Such an arrangement would overcome the crudeness and inflexibility of laws, the problem pointed to in the earlier discussion of returning another's property; it would best incorporate the knowledge needed to help people, the problem raised in the search for the art of justice, or the first part of Socrates' critique of justice as helping friends and harming enemies; and it would seem never to cause undue harm, the problem raised in the second and third parts of Socrates' critique. Yet, having rejected the interpretation that giving to each what is owed means helping friends and harming enemies, Socrates does not offer this alternative. Instead, he asks that another definition of justice be proposed (336a9–10). Why doesn't he say that justice is giving to each what is fitting?

In a way, Socrates *does* say that justice is giving to each what is fitting. At least he does so later on. The bulk of the *Republic* can be seen as the working out, if only on the scale of a particular city, of this view of justice, with the requirement in particular that the wise have absolute rule. Yet that attempt to put this view of justice into action, so to speak, in speech may be intended partly to show the impossibility of doing so in deed.[38] Of course, it would be necessary to study the whole *Republic* to see all of the reasons for that impossibility. But already here in Book One we can see at least some of the problems—and these problems may help to explain why Socrates does not offer in Book One the same "solution" to the problem of justice that he does in the bulk of the *Republic* (where the demands of Glaucon and Adeimantus—and even of Polemarchus too—place him under greater compulsion to do so: see 357a1ff., 449a1ff.).

The most massive problem, or the most massive obstacle standing in the way of the arrangement necessary to give to each what is fitting, is something we have already observed a couple of times in connection with Socrates' arguments that moved in the direction of giving to each what is fitting (see pages 43–44 and 48 above). In short, political life, given its constraints, makes impossible its own transformation into something as different as it would have to be to give to each what is fitting. Even leaving aside the impossible hope that the division of the world into cities, or nations, could be overcome (as it would have to be to give to *each* what is fitting), the measures required to give to each what is fitting on even the more limited scale of a particular city would never be allowed. The absolute rule of the wise, in particular, and all of the reforms that would be necessary for the establishment of such rule, would never be permitted by the unwise, who could not be expected to see that the rule of the wise would be good for them and who are always more numerous and stronger than the wise. Indeed, the opening scene of the *Republic* (the seizing of Socrates: 327a1–328b3) is a playful presentation, and the bulk of the *Republic* a thematic treatment, of the limits of wisdom in the face of the political power of the unwise.

But in addition to this obvious obstacle facing the rule of the wise and therewith the possibility of giving to each what is fitting, there is another less obvious but perhaps more troubling problem: Would the wise be willing to rule? For while a case can be made that it would be good for the others, the unwise, to be ruled by the wise, it might not be so beneficial for the wise themselves to spend their time and energy attending to the problems and needs of everyone else. The

---

38. For the clearest indication consider 540e5–541a7. The most extensive argument that Socrates' "City-in-Speech" is not meant to be an actually practicable proposal is Strauss, *The City and Man*, especially pp. 124–127.

rule of the wise may seem to be the solution by which each can be given what is fitting, what is good for them, and justice can thereby be unambiguously good. But we have to ask whether this "solution" would not come at the expense of at least some of those involved, and perhaps the most important ones.

Now, by way of conclusion, I want to consider a possible response to this last point. For perhaps it could be said that this is hard luck for the wise, that if their rule is what is required for the good of everyone else, then they have an obligation to rule (consider 519c8–520e3). Here we should recall, again, that we were originally led to the view that justice ought to be giving to each what is fitting, and therefore that the wise ought to rule, by the importance, affirmed implicitly by Cephalus and Polemarchus, of the thought that justice is good. Since Cephalus and Polemarchus proved unwilling to call something harmful or bad just, we can even say that they demanded that justice be good. Yet there was an ambiguity in that demand that we have not yet considered: good *for whom?* In Socrates' initial example of the mad friend demanding his weapons back, it went without saying that it was better for both the madman and the friend holding the weapons that the weapons not be returned. In one of his subsequent examples, however, Socrates secured Polemarchus' agreement to the specific statement that it would not be just if the return of gold (in that case) to a friend harmed *both* the giver (the returner of the gold) *and* the receiver (332a11–b4). That raises the question: What if it harmed only one of them, either the giver or the receiver? The case of the giver is more important. Is the demand that justice be good a demand—or does it include the demand—that it be good for the giver, that is, for the just man himself? To return to the case of the rule of the wise, we might want to say that it is just for the wise man to sacrifice his own good for the sake of everyone else. But can we really maintain the claim that he is *rightfully obligated* to do so? What would that mean? Among other things, it would mean that we would have to require as a just obligation something that would be harmful to the most just man, something that would seriously detract from his happiness. And I think it is correct to say that as much as we find it unacceptable, or unjust, if justice harms its recipients, so—indeed even more so—do we find it unacceptable, or unjust, if justice harms those who are the doers of justice, those who are the most just. Don't we say, after all, that it is unjust when the just suffer, and that for justice to be done they must prosper instead (see 334d5–11)? And don't we show a concern that justice be good for the just man either by believing that it is ultimately good for its own sake to be just (see 335c1– d10), or by expecting to be rewarded for our justice (see 330d4–331b7)? So central to our opinions about justice is the goodness of justice— that is, the conviction that it is good for us to be just—that these opinions attest to the importance of our concern for our own good. It would thus be on grounds ultimately acknowledged by justice itself, we could say, that the wise man could turn his back on rule, if he were convinced that there is a better way of life (consider, e.g., 347b5–d8, 517c7–d2; see also Plato, *Apology of Socrates* 31d5–32a2, 38a1–8).[39]

---

39. This line of thought might seem to be contradicted by Socrates' own argument later in the *Republic* that the philosophers who have seen the Idea of the Good would justly be compelled to return to the Cave and rule there (see 519c8–520e3). Socrates makes a two-part argument in that passage. First, he reminds Glaucon of an argument made earlier in the *Republic* that the law should aim at the good of the whole city, not the good of any one part of it. Second, Socrates argues that, while it would be fitting for philosophers to avoid rule in other cities, in their city, that is, in the City-in-Speech of the *Republic*, the philosophers owe it to the city to rule since the city has reared them and educated them to be what they are. However, there are several difficulties with this argument. The most obvious difficulty is that Socrates acknowledges that at least the second part of the argument applies *only* to the City-in-Speech; he thus implies, and even states (520a9–b2), that philosophers are *not* obligated to rule in any other city—that is, in any city that actually exists. As for the first part of his argument, while it is true that Socrates argues not only in this passage but also elsewhere in the *Republic* that the good of the whole city is more important than the good of any part (see, e.g., 420b3–421c6), this argument must be weighed against the whole project of the *Republic*, which is to show that justice is good for the individual. Moreover, one must ask whether the insistence on the happiness of the whole over the happiness of the parts is ultimately coherent. How can "the whole" be happy without happy parts? Aristotle raises this objection to Socrates' argument in his critique of the *Republic* in Book Two of the *Politics*, where he points out that happiness is not same kind of thing as evenness, which can exist in the whole but not in its parts (1264b15–21). Socrates' suggestion that the philosophers whom he is discussing would have to be *compelled* to rule suggests that they too would not find his argument in Book Seven fully convincing (see 519c8–d2; see again 347b5–d8). Finally, it is noteworthy that Glaucon objects, at least initially, to Socrates' suggestion that the philosophers should be compelled to rule; he thus shows a concern, as a just man, with the happiness of the just: "Are we going to do them an injustice, and make them live worse lives when it is possible for them to live better ones?" (519d8–9).

Chapter 2

Thrasymachus and the Question of the Goodness of Justice

Once Socrates and Polemarchus have joined forces against the view that justice is helping friends and harming enemies, there is a pause in the conversation as Socrates awaits the next attempt to say what justice is (336a9–b4). This pause enables Thrasymachus to make his dramatic entry into the conversation, finally bursting in as he had been trying to do for some time (336b1–6). Now, Socrates' failure to return to the suggestion that justice is giving to each what is fitting at the end of his discussion with Polemarchus has led us to reflect on the thought or conviction that has, in one way or another, driven much of the discussion thus far: the conviction that justice is good. And to state briefly the most important thing we have just found, this conviction not only applies to the recipients of justice, that is, those whom the just man seeks to help, but it extends also to the practitioner of justice, the just man himself. However, it should be emphasized that this is a point whose significance we have come to see only at the end of our study of Socrates' discussion with Polemarchus and only on the basis of a reflection prompted but not made explicit by the text itself. If the conviction that justice is good has driven much of the conversation thus far, it has been primarily the conviction that justice is good for its recipients, or, in other words, for *others*, that has been the focus of attention. The goodness of justice for the just man himself, while certainly not denied, has remained more or less implicit; or, perhaps better to say, it has remained *assumed* (consider, though, 335c4–5). With Thrasymachus' entry, however, this assump-

57

tion is soon to receive an extreme shaking and the goodness of justice for the just will undergo perhaps its most famous attack.

Thrasymachus' attack on justice will initiate a crucial turn in Book One, one that will affect the entire *Republic*. Whereas the focus of the discussion up to now has been on what justice is, with Socrates leading the search for the true definition of justice, at a certain point in Socrates' discussion with Thrasymachus the guiding question will shift to the question of whether justice is good—and Socrates' role will shift accordingly from leading the search for justice to defending the goodness of justice. But this turn should raise a number of questions. In addition to the questions that we will have to raise about the character of Socrates' defense of justice, and the question Socrates himself will raise of how one can defend something before one has successfully discovered what it is, our study in the preceding chapter should prompt us to raise the following question. Socrates' exchanges with Cephalus and Polemarchus were driven, as we have stressed, by the conviction or the assumption that justice must be good, an assumption that we have just concluded ultimately means good for the practitioner as well as the recipient of justice. These exchanges, to put this another way, were driven by the thought that justice would not be justice if it were not good. The turn, however, to the question of the goodness of justice *as a question* (see 344d5–345b3, 347e2–348b4), seems to imply that justice *could* be bad. Can justice not be good and still be justice? The turn to the question of the goodness of justice will force us to consider another question as well: Should justice be judged by and hence subordinated to a standard other than justice itself?

The Opening Exchange Between Thrasymachus and Socrates (336b1–338b9)

Socrates' conversation with Thrasymachus takes the form of an extended quarrel in which Socrates stands as the defender of justice against Thrasymachus' critique. This critique and thus this quarrel begin in earnest at 338c1–2, where Thrasymachus first defines justice as the advantage of the stronger. Preceding this definition of justice, however, and standing as a kind of prelude to their main quarrel, is a brief opening exchange between Thrasymachus and Socrates. Thrasymachus, we see here, enters the conversation of the *Republic* not in the first place to give his own answer to the question of what justice is, but rather to demand that Socrates do so.

Thrasymachus' insistence that Socrates give a definition of justice is part of a larger charge against Socrates (and partly against Polemarchus too)[1] prompted by what Thrasymachus sees as the foolishness and lack of seriousness of the earlier search for justice (336b8–c2). According to Thrasymachus, Socrates has been exploiting the fact that it is easier to ask questions than to answer them and has been gratifying his love of honor by refuting others rather than genuinely trying to discover what justice is (336c2–6). Irritated by Socrates' behavior, Thrasymachus insists that Socrates now become more serious and say what he himself thinks justice is. He warns Socrates, however, against giving several specific answers. Socrates is not to say the just is the needful, the helpful, the profitable, the gainful, or the advantageous, because he will not accept "such inanities" (336c6–d4). For all of Thrasymachus' fame, or rather notoriety, as an immoral critic of justice, this is not exactly how he first appears as he makes his entry into the conversation. Thrasymachus is angry and behaves so fiercely that Socrates compares him to a beast (336b5, d5–7). But his anger and fierceness seem to be those of moral indignation. And such indignation, disagreeing with Socrates' recent argument with Polemarchus that it is never just to harm anyone, seeks punishment as the proper retribution for wrongdoing (compare, in particular, 336b5–6 and 337d2 with 335d11–e6).

If Thrasymachus' attack is in fact driven by moral indignation, Socrates' response is of particular interest. In an attempt to assuage Thrasymachus' anger at the earlier search for justice, Socrates tells Thrasymachus to consider whether he and Polemarchus, who of course would never voluntarily hinder their search for gold, would be willing to do so when searching for justice, something more precious (or more honored: *timiōteron*) than much gold (336e2–10). Socrates appeals here once again to the assumption he has been appealing to throughout the dialogue, the assumption, namely, that

---

1. Although Thrasymachus addresses his accusation to Socrates by name, it begins with two questions (336b8–c2) in which Thrasymachus uses the plural "you" (*humas, humin*). The second question in particular is clearly directed at Polemarchus as well as Socrates.

justice is something good (consider, however, the ambiguity of *timiōteron*). And on the assumption that justice is something good, Socrates' argument that Thrasymachus' anger is unwarranted seems to be reasonable: if justice is something good, then the failure to find it is a harm to oneself and as such must be attributed to ignorance or incompetence, not to deliberate or voluntary wrongdoing; for this reason, and since anyone failing to find something good is suffering already, it is more appropriate to pity than to hate or seek to harm those who make such mistakes (336e2–337a2).[2]

Thrasymachus, however, is not convinced: "Heracles! Here's that typical irony of Socrates—I knew it, and I predicted to these others that you wouldn't be willing to answer, that you would be ironic and go to all lengths not to answer if someone asked you something" (337a3–7).[3] By scorning Socrates' argument as he does, taking it to be an ironic attempt to avoid answering, Thrasymachus implicitly reasserts his demand that Socrates say what he himself thinks justice is. Socrates must thus speak explicitly to why he is unwilling, as he apparently is, to do so.

Socrates ultimately escapes Thrasymachus' demand that he give his own answer to the question of what justice is; but he does so less by the force of argument than by tempting Thrasymachus into answering in his place. Socrates' defense of his unwillingness to answer moves between two excuses. He argues, in the first place, that he cannot answer because Thrasymachus has prohibited certain (and, he implies, the correct) answers (337a8–c1). Then he goes on to argue that he cannot answer because he does not know what justice is and would not even have an opinion until he has examined the matter (337c9–d4). These two excuses, however, undercut one another, the first resting on the premise that Socrates has at least an

---

2. See pages 50–51 above. And see again Plato, *Laws* 731c1–d3, *Apology of Socrates* 25c5–26a7, and *Cleitophon* 407d2–e2.

3. Socrates' argument is read by Thrasymachus as an ironic attempt to avoid answering presumably because the argument contains an implicit claim of ignorance. It is worth noting that although Thrasymachus attacks Socrates for not being serious in his efforts to discover what justice is, questioning whether Socrates truly cares about knowing the answer, he also thinks that Socrates has at least an opinion about what justice is. Thrasymachus is angry at Socrates for his unwillingness to state this opinion; it would seem, in fact, that it is what he perceives as Socrates' dissembling or lack of frankness that has most provoked Thrasymachus.

idea of what justice is (such that he knows Thrasymachus' prohibition to be a genuine obstacle), the second denying any such idea (cf. 337e4–7). Nor will Socrates' excuses suffice from a practical standpoint: Socrates admits that he could not reasonably be expected to respect Thrasymachus' prohibition if it prohibited what seemed to him to be the correct answer (337c3–6), and Socrates' appeal to his ignorance will never be convincing, at least not to Thrasymachus who has shown that he thinks any such appeal on Socrates' part is ironic.[4]

Socrates escapes answering only because Thrasymachus thinks, as Socrates tells us, that he has a "very fine" answer of his own, one which Thrasymachus himself says is better than those he has prohibited (338a5–7, 337d1–2). And by dangling the promise of both money as well as praise before Thrasymachus, playing on Thrasymachus' love of money and especially of honor, Socrates is able to get Thrasymachus to give up the attempt to force him to answer in the anticipation that greater gains lie in answering in Socrates' place.[5] Socrates gets himself off the hook, then, without having adequately responded to the charges against him.

The only sound argument that Socrates seems to have made in this opening exchange with Thrasymachus is his first argument, the one which, if not providing an adequate defense of his present unwillingness to answer, at least seems to make a reasonable case that Thrasymachus' anger at Socrates and Polemarchus' earlier behavior is unwarranted. Yet there is a difficulty, or at least a complexity, with even this argument. As we recall, it rests on the assump-

---

4. Socrates' declaration of ignorance is unlikely to be acceptable also from a civic point of view. According to a suggestion of Strauss and Bloom (see *The City and Man*, pp. 74–76; "Interpretive Essay," pp. 326–327), Thrasymachus imitates the city in its hostility to Socrates. While I am reluctant to extend the equation of Thrasymachus and the city very far (Strauss and Bloom take it further than this one point), it surely makes sense to say that the city cannot simply welcome Socrates' (frequent) declarations that he does not know what justice is. Apart from the difficulty that one who does not know what justice is would seem to have a hard time being just, this declaration has the simpler problem that it implies a refusal to accept the city's view of justice.

5. See 337d6–10, 338a1–6, b5–9. On Thrasymachus' love of honor see also Nichols, p. 49; Benardete, pp. 22–23; Jacob Howland, *The Republic: The Odyssey of Philosophy* (New York: Twayne Publishers, 1993), p. 66.

tion that justice, like gold, is something good. We are soon to see, however, how problematic this assumption is; it is the very thing Thrasymachus will soon call into question. Thrasymachus will soon claim that justice is nothing like gold. Gold, after all, is one of the preeminent private goods, the possession of which seems clearly good for its possessor; it is a good, moreover, that helps its possessor in his desire to get other goods. Justice, by contrast, is more obviously good for those whom the just man helps than for the just man himself; unlike gold, it can be a limit on its possessor's desire for other goods. For reasons such as these, Thrasymachus will argue that one is better off freeing oneself from the restraints of justice. By claiming that the unjust life is better than the just life, Thrasymachus will reject in an obvious and radical way the assumption that justice is good. Lest we think, however, that Thrasymachus' radical immoralism is simply the rejection or the utter opposite of ordinary decent opinion, we should bear in mind that there is at least one respect, one brought out by this opening exchange, in which such opinion seems to agree with Thrasymachus rather than Socrates. As reasonable as Socrates' argument may be on the assumption that justice is good—an assumption borrowed from ordinary decent opinion—that argument leads to the conclusion that one ought not to get angry at or even blame wrongdoers. This conclusion, however, is deeply at odds with the ordinary understanding of the proper attitude toward crime and punishment. On this point at least, the ordinary moral outlook seems to be reflected more in the actions and demeanor of Thrasymachus than of Socrates.[6]

Thrasymachus' Definition of Justice (338c1–339e8)

Abandoning the demand that Socrates say what he thinks justice is, Thrasymachus gives his own definition, the one for which he is famous: justice is the advantage of the stronger. Actually, that is not precisely what he says. He says that justice, or "the just," is "*nothing other than* the advantage of the stronger" (338c1–2, emphasis added). Stated in this way, Thrasymachus' definition seems from the

---

6. See Strauss, *The City and Man*, p. 77: "The immoral Thrasymachus is morally indignant whereas moral Socrates is, or pretends to be, merely afraid."

beginning to be set against claims or beliefs or hopes that justice is something more than what he thinks it is. It is not immediately clear, however, exactly what these claims or beliefs or hopes are. Thrasymachus' definition seems to express the conclusion of a line of reasoning (see 339a2–3). But what is this line of reasoning? And what is he arguing against? As Socrates suggests, by stating only his conclusion Thrasymachus has not yet made it clear what he means (338c4–d2, d5–6).

Urged to explain his definition, Thrasymachus turns Socrates' attention to cities and how they are ruled. Cities, Thrasymachus observes, come in types: some are tyrannies, others democracies, and still others aristocracies (338d7–8). This division of cities into various types is based, though, on a characteristic they all share: in each city one group, the ruling group, dominates the whole city (338d10). And this in turn explains, according to Thrasymachus, not only why cities come in types but why laws do as well:

> Each ruling group sets down the laws with a view to its own advantage: a democracy [sets down] democratic laws; a tyranny, tyrannical laws; and the others do the same sort of thing. And having set this down, namely, their own advantage, they declare this to be just for the ruled, and they punish the man who strays from this as a lawbreaker and a doer of injustice. (338e1–6)

In this statement, Thrasymachus does not contest the declarations of the ruling groups in the various cities according to which justice consists in obedience to the laws they have set down. In this respect, Thrasymachus' position is not so heterodoxical; he holds the view, to state it in its most respectable form, that the just is the legal.[7]

---

7. The question of whether Thrasymachus equates the just with the legal is a source of much dispute. Primarily on the basis of later statements of Thrasymachus, especially at 340d1–341a4 and 343c1–d1, many have argued that Thrasymachus' understanding of justice as the advantage of the stronger does not rest on an equation of the just and the legal, or, more generally, that it is not based on a reflection about the law. See Cross and Woozely, pp. 32–36; Terence Irwin, *Plato's Ethics* (New York: Oxford University Press, 1995), pp. 174–175, and p. 377, n. 24; Kimon Lycos, *Plato on Justice and Power* (Albany: State University of New York Press, 1987) pp. 46–51, 56; T. Y. Henderson, "In Defense of Thrasymachus," *American Philosophical Quarterly* 7 (1970): 218–228; Friedländer, p. 61; Demetrius Hardgo-

A problem would seem to arise, however, for anyone who follows the rulers in each city in equating justice with obedience to their laws, for there are many cities and their laws differ. It would seem, then, that justice varies from city to city, that it takes as many forms as there are cities or at least types of cities. Yet Thrasymachus wants not so much to stress this variability in justice as to explain how justice is "everywhere the same thing." He completes his explanation to Socrates:

> This, then, best of men, is what I mean—in every city the same thing is just, the advantage of the established ruling group. This presumably dominates, so it follows for the one who reasons correctly that justice is everywhere the same thing, the advantage of the stronger. (338e6–339a4, emphasis added)

According to Thrasymachus, the manifest variety among the laws of the various cities is less important than the sameness of purpose that underlies all laws and thus underlies justice in whatever form it might take. In fact, the very reason that Thrasymachus calls attention to the variety among the laws of the various types of cities is that he takes this variety to be a reflection of the sameness of their purpose: laws vary because they are all made for the advantage of the stronger, an advantage that varies from place to place depending on who the stronger are. In every city justice takes a different form, but it does so precisely because it has the same root, for in each city a particular

---

poulus, "Thrasymachus and Legalism," *Phronesis* 18 (1973): 204–208; G. B. Kerferd, "The Doctrine of Thrasymachus in Plato's *Republic*," *Durham University Journal* 9 (1947–1948): 19–27, and "Thrasymachus and Justice: A Reply," *Phronesis* 9 (1964): 12–16. It seems to me, however, that before considering any shifts Thrasymachus might go on to make in his position, it is best to begin from his original explication quoted above, and here the just does seem equivalent to the legal. On this side of the dispute, consider Annas, *An Introduction*, pp. 35–38; Benardete, pp. 22–24; Nettleship, pp. 27–32; Reeve, pp. 11–15; F. E. Sparshott, "Socrates and Thrasymachus," *The Monist* 50 (1966): 421–459, pp. 422–432; Sallis, p. 336; Bloom, pp. 326–328; Strauss, *The City and Man*, p. 75; George Hourani, "Thrasymachus' Definition of Justice in Plato's *Republic*," *Phronesis* 7 (1962): 110–120; and J. P. Maguire, "Thrasymachus . . . or Plato?" *Phronesis* 16 (1971): 142–163, pp. 147–151.

group, be it the poor, the rich, or one man, has gained dominance, set down laws to its (or his) own advantage, and declared that it is just for the others, the ruled, to obey these laws.

Now, by this point it should be becoming clear that even if he is presenting what in a certain respect is a common and respectable position, insofar as he follows the equation of the just and the legal, Thrasymachus does not hold a common and respectable view of justice in all respects. Indeed, Thrasymachus himself asserts his unconventionality: his is the understanding of "one who reasons correctly" (339a2–3), and again, justice is "*nothing other than* the advantage of the stronger." But what exactly differentiates Thrasymachus' position from the ordinary political view? To begin with, let us say that while Thrasymachus begins from the claim of each city that its laws are just, he does not accord this claim the same status or meaning that the cities do. As we have seen, Thrasymachus judges the laws of the various cities by their origin and purpose. He points out that the laws are always made by the group that has gained dominance in each city. This ruling group, then, is the source of justice, establishing it through their insistence that the ruled have a duty to obey the laws they have set down. As the source of justice, however, the rulers themselves are not bound by justice; the only standard guiding their actions is their own good. This means that justice has a root that is not itself just, or, stated differently, justice according to Thrasymachus is a kind of fraud: the rulers, who are guided by nothing other than their own good, impose a different standard on others and claim that the ruled are obligated to serve them.

But aren't the rulers bound by the laws as well? And is it really true that the rulers are guided by nothing other than their own good when they make the laws? The second of these objections is more fundamental, since Thrasymachus could respond to the first by arguing that even though the laws in what are thought to be healthy cities are applicable to the rulers as well as the ruled, the decisive point is who makes them and whose good they serve: there is no crucial difference, by Thrasymachus' account, between the rule of law and a tyrannical decree because lying behind any law is the equivalent of a tyrannical decree. In addition and more simply, Thrasymachus could respond that the rulers are not bound by the laws they set down inasmuch as they can always change the laws.[8]

But what about Thrasymachus' claim that rulers are guided by nothing other than their own good? This is his most important claim, and it is also the one the rulers themselves would most object to. For what the rulers in the various cities mean when they call their laws "just" is not only that the ruled have a duty to obey these laws but also that the laws serve a *just purpose*. When they claim that their laws are just, and so too when they claim that they themselves deserve to rule not merely by superior force but by right, the rulers claim to serve a standard of justice prior to their laws and higher than their own good. The most well-known standard to which the rulers point is the common good: laws and rulers are said to be just because, or insofar as, they serve the common good.[9] Here, then, would seem to be the heart of the disagreement between Thrasymachus and the ordinary political view, for while Thrasymachus has not yet explicitly denied the existence of a common good in cities, he has asserted that the good that guides the laws in each city is always a particular or private one.[10]

---

8. In his explanation of his definition, Thrasymachus speaks twice of the various kinds of regimes. In the first instance (338d7–8), he mentions tyranny, democracy, and aristocracy, in that order. In the second instance (338e2–3), he mentions democracy, tyranny, and "the others," dropping specific mention of aristocracy and switching the places of tyranny and democracy. Thrasymachus' emphasis on tyranny and democracy, and their seeming interchangeability in his account, is an implicit assertion that democracy (the regime in which freedom and the rule of law would seem to have their most natural home) is at root no different than tyranny (the regime least characterized by freedom and the rule of law).

Although Aristotle would neither agree with this assertion nor accept Thrasymachus' implicit critique of the significance of the rule of law more generally, consider Aristotle's remarks at *Politics* 1281a34–38; since laws are made by regimes, the rule of law is not by itself a sufficient answer to the kind of difficulties Thrasymachus raises.

9. Compare Aristotle, *Nicomachean Ethics* 1129b17–19, *Politics* 1279a17–21, 1282b15–17.

10. Sparshott writes: "The most striking and consistent feature of [Thrasymachus'] thought is that he construes all encounters between groups and individuals as conflicts . . . That some arrangements may exist for the *common* good is simply beyond his grasp" (p. 427; emphasis in the text). Sparshott, however, is somewhat unfair to Thrasymachus: Thrasymachus is not oblivious to the possibility of a common good; he doubts, rather, that one actually exists.

Once Thrasymachus has finished his explanation of his definition of justice, Socrates says that he now sees what Thrasymachus is
arguing (339a5). That is not to say, however, that he is convinced:
"But whether [what you say] is true or not, I shall try to learn"
(339a5–6, see also b2–5). Given the importance that we have just
sketched of the common good as a standard of justice, and thus the
significance of Thrasymachus' denial that this standard ever guides
the actions of rulers, we might expect that Socrates will appeal now
to this standard and attempt to defend it against Thrasymachus'
claims. We might expect Socrates to defend the claims of rulers to act
for the sake of the common good, or at least to argue that this is true
of at least *some* rulers. By arguing this latter point, Socrates could
thereby argue that, contrary to Thrasymachus' assertions, not all
laws and not all rulers are morally equivalent—that is, lines can be
drawn between just and unjust laws and just and unjust rulers.[11] At
the very least, we might expect Socrates to argue, as a perhaps more
limited defense of the common good, that even if rulers are pursuing
their own good, they must act in a way that indirectly benefits the
ruled as well. By implying that rulers make laws that benefit *only*
themselves, Thrasymachus has surely been too rash and extreme in
ignoring the mutual interest the rulers and the ruled have in the
preservation of some degree of peace, order, and stability.

At least initially, however, Socrates makes none of these arguments. Instead, he begins with the seemingly minor objection that
rulers sometimes make mistakes. He does indeed get Thrasymachus
to admit that it is possible to distinguish between "correct" and
"incorrect" laws, but the standard is whether or not a given law is in
fact good for the rulers who set it down. Since rulers are fallible, they
sometimes set down "incorrect" laws that turn out to be to their dis-
advantage (339c1–9). Given that rulers makes such mistakes, Socrates argues, Thrasymachus cannot maintain as he wants to both that it
is just for the ruled to obey the laws set down by the rulers and that
justice is the advantage of the stronger. When the rulers, the stronger,
make such mistakes, it will be just for the ruled, who must nonethe-

---

11. Compare Plato, *Laws* 715b2–6 and especially Aristotle, *Politics* 1279a17–
21 where Aristotle makes looking to "the common advantage" the basis of his
famous distinction between "correct" regimes "according to what is simply just"
and "deviations."

less obey the rulers' laws or commands, to do what is disadvantageous for the stronger (339b7–e8).

Rulers in the Strict Sense (340a1-343a2)

In order to begin to understand why Socrates starts with this undoubtedly true but nonetheless seemingly minor argument about the fallibility of rulers, we need to look a bit more at Thrasymachus' position, and in particular at a side of it we have so far neglected. Socrates' argument surprises and dissatisfies us because it does not seem to speak to what we have taken to be the most important and troubling aspect of what Thrasymachus has said: his claim that rulers do not act for the sake of the common good. But there is more to Thrasymachus' position, or, perhaps better, more to Thrasymachus himself, than this claim. Or, to put this yet another way, this claim can be read in two different and seemingly opposed ways, both of which are somehow intended by Thrasymachus.

We have said that by Thrasymachus' account justice is a kind of fraud. This sounds like, and it is, an accusation of the rulers: they are the culprits in this fraud; they are the ones using "justice" to exploit the ruled. Yet while Thrasymachus may be blaming and even trying to expose the rulers—thus explaining his great openness and boldness[12]—there is another sense in which his presentation of justice is

---

12. It is sometimes suggested that Thrasymachus is led to be so forthright in declaring his thoughts about justice, not by any indignation he may feel, but by his desire as a teacher of rhetoric to attract students; Thrasymachus' impending downfall, according to this interpretation, is caused by a fatal tension between his need to advertise and the reserve that prudence would otherwise dictate (See, e.g., Sallis, pp. 338–39, 343–44, Howland, pp. 69–75). However, the inadequacy or at least the incompleteness of this explanation is indicated by several facts. The first is Thrasymachus' anger. It is true that Thrasymachus' anger has been directed primarily at Socrates himself. But it has been prompted by what Thrasymachus has viewed as Socrates' sophisticated manipulation of justice, his sycophantic pretext that he has been searching for justice when he has really been pursuing his own honor (see again 336b1–338b3, 338d3–4, and see 340d1–341c3). Moreover, Thrasymachus will become even more angry—and accordingly even more open and extreme in his arguments—when a certain argument of Socrates about the selflessness of artisans and rulers later convinces him that Socrates is not in fact the sycophant he initially appeared to be but is himself naively taken in by justice (see 342e6–344c8). Yet why

meant as a praise and even a vindication of the rulers. The rulers, after all, are the ones who are not taken in by justice; they are the ones who are clear-sighted in their pursuit of their own good. If justice is a fraud, if it is a standard used by the rulers merely to get others to do their bidding, the rulers are indeed the culprits, but they are also the ones drawing the reasonable conclusion and acting prudently. Socrates' argument shifts the focus of attention to this latter aspect of Thrasymachus' position, or to this side of his character, especially to his admiration of the knowledge rulers must possess if they are to see and to secure their own good.[13]

Thrasymachus follows this shift and even accentuates it in his response to Socrates' argument. As Cleitophon brings out in a brief exchange with Polemarchus, an exchange in which Polemarchus stands in briefly for Socrates and Cleitophon for Thrasymachus (340a1–b9), there is an easy way out of the contradiction Socrates has pointed to in Thrasymachus' position. To solve the difficulty that if rulers make mistakes justice is not always the advantage of the stronger, all Thrasymachus has to add is that the advantage of the stronger that dictates what justice is need not be their true advantage, but only what the stronger *believe* to be to their advantage (340b6–8). Thrasymachus, however, emphatically rejects this qualification of

---

would such apparent naiveté provoke, rather than delight, Thrasymachus? One must explain his desire to deprive the just of their innocence, a desire that a thoroughly unjust and calculating man would not feel (see especially 343d1–e7). As for the response that Thrasymachus attempts to "enlighten" Socrates only because his eyes are on prospective pupils in the crowd listening to their conversation, it should also be noted, in addition to the fact of his anger, that Thrasymachus never boasts of the power of his art of rhetoric. Unlike his counterpart Gorgias, a more famous and self-promoting teacher of rhetoric who is at the same time far more reserved about his own view of justice, Thrasymachus never so much as mentions rhetoric in his conversation with Socrates (compare especially *Gorgias* 452d5–e8, 455d6–456c6; consider, however, *Republic* 340d1–341a4). Admittedly, Socrates himself has spoken at one point of Thrasymachus' desire to win a good reputation (338a5–6); but this would seem in context to refer to a reputation less as a skilled rhetorician than as a man willing—as Thrasymachus complains Socrates is not—to speak the truth about justice (consider again 336b8–337e3, 338b1–c3).

13. By emphasizing the more "Machiavellian" side of Thrasymachus, Socrates in a way encourages Thrasymachus to make the case for injustice. If it is Thrasymachus who will bear the explicit responsibility for opening up the question of the goodness of justice, Socrates helps here to provide at least a gentle push.

the advantage of the stronger (340c6–7). He chooses instead to try to escape his contradiction by redefining, or, as he puts it, by making more precise, who the stronger are. Whereas Thrasymachus had earlier spoken of rulers in the ordinary sense, rulers who are of course fallible (see 338d7–339a4, 339c1–9), he now insists on considering only rulers "in the strict sense." Rulers in the strict sense are like craftsmen in the strict sense, who are infallible insofar as they are what they are called (340d1–341a4). Rather than taking, then, what would seem to be the simplest path to preserving the essentials of his presentation of justice, Thrasymachus turns out to be more concerned with defending the rulers, at least those rulers who have the knowledge necessary to see and to secure their own good. As we will see, however, although knowledge is necessary to see and to secure one's own good, Thrasymachus proves not to have given enough thought to the way in which knowledge appears to direct one to something other than one's own good.

Thrasymachus develops the idea of rulers in the strict sense in his longest speech thus far (340d1–341a4). In this speech, he begins with the analogy of craftsmen, those who possess knowledge of the various arts. Actually, to be more precise, he begins negatively, by speaking of those who are sometimes said to be craftsmen but do not truly deserve the names by which they are called. The man who makes mistakes in his attempt to cure the sick, for example, should not be called a doctor, nor should the one who errs in his calculations be called a calculator (*logistikon*). It is only in our loose manner of speaking that we use titles like "doctor," "calculator," or "grammarian" in such cases—that we say, for instance, "The doctor made a mistake." If we were to be precise, says Thrasymachus, that is, if we were to speak strictly rather than loosely, we would never call one who makes mistakes by the name of a craftsman, since insofar as he is what we call him, a craftsman never makes mistakes (340d2–e3). "For the man who makes mistakes," Thrasymachus explains, "makes them due to a lack of knowledge, and in this respect he is not a craftsman" (340e3–4). And just as craftsmen can be seen as rulers of sorts, inasmuch as they rule over their subject matter, so too rulers (of men) are at least analogous to craftsmen, since rulers in the strict sense are possessors of knowledge (340e4–6). Hence: "the ruler, insofar as he is ruling, never makes mistakes, and never making mistakes, he sets down what is best for himself—and this is what must be done by the ruled" (340e8–341a2).

Now, Thrasymachus claims that this speech is consistent with what he has been saying from the beginning, and indeed it does restore the standing of "the advantage of the stronger" by declaring that it is impossible for rulers in the strict sense, the truly stronger, to do what is disadvantageous for themselves (340a3–4). However, if Thrasymachus has preserved his definition of justice with this speech, he has been able to do so only by transforming its meaning. Thrasymachus first explained his definition by pointing to the practices and laws of actual cities and to the everyday facts of political power. Now, by contrast, he has replaced the commonsensical understanding that rulers are all those in power, with the paradoxical claim that only knowledge can make one truly a ruler. This means, among other things, that Thrasymachus can no longer claim that the just is everywhere the legal—at least not without an extremely paradoxical understanding of the legal. Moreover, although Thrasymachus still maintains that the ruled must do what the rulers set down (341a2, see also b6–8), it is hard to see, now that he has severed the necessary connection between rule and actually having power in a city, exactly who "the ruled" are and why it would be just for them to obey the rulers. Where before the "right of the stronger" seemed to rest primarily on a fait accompli—along the lines of "The strong do what they can, the weak suffer what they must" (allowing some room for fraud to accompany force)—it is no longer clear what the basis of the obedience of "the weak" to "the strong" would be.[14]

It is important to notice that Thrasymachus has thus moved to what is almost a new position, and that it is one that does not seem to be fully coherent. Among other reasons this is important is that it is against *this* position that Socrates now argues (see especially 341b3–8). In what follows, Socrates will refute the view that rulers in the strict sense pursue their own advantage. We should note in advance, however, that this refutation will leave unaddressed the practice of the so-called rulers of ordinary speech, that is to say, the practice of

---

14. Several commentators have noted the shifts in Thrasymachus' position and the perplexity of his present view. See, for example, Sallis, p. 338; Bloom, pp. 328–329; Annas, *An Introduction*, pp. 42–43; Benardete, p. 23; Reeve, pp. 13–15; Friedländer, p. 62; Strauss, *The City and Man*, pp. 75–80.

almost all rulers who ever rule in actual cities. The only way in which Socrates' argument about rulers in the strict sense can be said to bear on or speak to ordinary political life and the claims with which Thrasymachus began (see again 338d7–339a4), is that it perhaps establishes a standard in light of which ordinary rulers might, if they in fact act as Thrasymachus says they do, be judged and criticized.

Bearing this in mind, let us turn to Socrates' argument, his second argument against Thrasymachus' definition of justice. Socrates' argument is a deft inversion of Thrasymachus' speech, in which Socrates uses the implications of the model provided by the craftsmen—or artisans, as they can be called following Socrates' use of the term *technē* (341d3ff.)—against Thrasymachus' claim that rulers, i.e., rulers in the strict sense, pursue only their own advantage.[15] For the arts, it turns out, provide a model not for the rulers' knowledge of and ability to secure their own good, but for the rulers' concern with the good of the ruled, or for what we might call the justice of the rulers.

It may seem strange that the arts should provide such a model. Didn't we *contrast* the arts and justice in our earlier consideration of Socrates' discussion with Polemarchus? Aren't the arts amoral, and wasn't Socrates' earlier use of the arts as an analogy for justice problematic because it abstracted from the just intention?[16] Without retracting our earlier statements, we must now acknowledge that the arts *do* bear a certain resemblance to justice. The devotion of the artisan to his art and the directedness of the art to its object is at least akin to the devotion and disinterestedness we take to be characteristic of the just man.[17] In fact, even Thrasymachus himself took a step in this direction in his speech, when he used the arts as a model for rulers who never make mistakes. Looking back for a moment at Thrasymachus' speech, we may notice that there was some ambiguity concerning exactly what a "mistake" consists of. In his concluding statement, Thrasymachus said of the ruler in the strict sense that "never making mistakes, he sets down what is best for himself," implying that a mistake would consist of the ruler doing something

---

15. See Sallis, p. 339; Bloom, p. 331; Strauss, *The City and Man*, pp. 78–79.

16. See pp. 36–37 above, and again 333e3–334a6 in particular.

17. Consider Sparshott's equation, commenting on this section, of "the scientific impulse" (impartiality) and "the impulse to justice" (pp. 440–441).

disadvantageous for the ruler himself (341a1–2; see also 339c7–9). This description of the ruler in the strict sense was arrived at, however, through the analogy of craftsmen, and there the mistake seemed to have a different character: the mistake rendering one undeserving of the title "doctor" was a mistake "concerning the sick," and the wrongly named calculator's mistake was "in calculation" (340d2–4). Especially in the case of the title "doctor," the right to this title seemed to hinge on one's ability to care correctly for something or someone other than oneself, to care correctly for *the sick*.

Not surprisingly, the doctor in the strict sense is precisely the example Socrates turns to first. The true doctor, he gets Thrasymachus to agree, is not a money-maker but a caretaker of the sick (341c4–8). Similarly, Socrates next speaks of the true pilot and gets Thrasymachus to agree that he is not a sailor but a ruler of sailors (341c9–d4).[18] Each of these two artisans, the doctor and the pilot, appears to possess an art that is naturally directed (*pephuken*) to the advantage of its objects, to patients in the one instance and sailors in the other (341d5–9).[19] And this directedness of these two arts to the advantage of objects other than the artisans themselves is meant to be characteristic of all the arts.

Socrates does not leave it, though, at this apparent natural directedness of the arts to the advantage of their objects. He also

---

18. The case of the pilot is similar but not exactly parallel to that of the doctor. The reason that it is not exactly parallel is that the pilot is, literally and figuratively, in the same boat as the sailors (341d1), and therefore an immediate common good would seem to exist between the pilot and the sailors that would seem not to exist between the doctor and his patient (hence the mention of moneymaking in the case of the doctor but not in the case of the pilot: money may serve to create an indirect or artificial common good). The claim that there is a full, positive common good between pilot and sailors rests, however, on the assumption that everyone on board wants or needs to sail where the boat is sailing. Compare Aristotle, *Politics* 1279a2–8.

19. I am reading *toutōn* at 341d5 as referring to the pilot's sailors and, less directly, to the doctor's patients. This is not absolutely clear in the Greek, but it is both the most likely and the most logical reading. See Adam, pp. 34–35. Allen, by contrast, takes it as referring to the artisans themselves, the doctor and the pilot (p. 97), but his reason for doing so—"there has been no mention yet of the objects whose welfare the arts secure"—is incorrect: see *tōn kamnontōn* at 341c6 and c8, *nautōn* at c9 and c11, and especially *tōn nautōn* at d3. Allen's reading would turn Socrates' argument upside down. See also 342d4–e4.

offers an account of what enables the arts to be so directed, or what the basis of this directedness is. Socrates offers this account through his explanation of the next question he puts to Thrasymachus, asking whether there is any advantage for each of the arts other than to be as perfect as possible (341d10–11). Socrates explains his question as follows. Each of the arts, he gets Thrasymachus to agree, was discovered or devised (*eurēmenē*, 341e5; *pareskeuasthē*, 341e7) because of a deficiency in something other than that art. The medical art, for example, was discovered or devised because the body is defective and in need of something to provide for its advantage (341e2–7). Socrates' question, as he now reformulates it, is whether, like the object whose defects it was developed to remedy, each of the various arts is itself defective and in need of an art, either another or its own, to remedy its defects. He gives Thrasymachus three alternatives to choose from (342a1–b7). The first is that each art is defective and needs another art to remedy its defects or to look after its advantage. (Those arts that assist other arts in this alternative are also defective and in need of other arts, which in turn need other arts, and so on infinitely.) The second alternative is that each art is defective but can remedy its own defects or look after its own advantage. And finally, the third alternative is that no art needs another art to look after it, nor does it have to look after itself, for by this alternative there is no defect or error in any art, but rather each art, "being correct, is unblemished and pure so long as it is precisely and entirely what it is." As Socrates surely could expect, Thrasymachus chooses this last alternative, by which the arts are perfect and without need. Thrasymachus may be reluctant to choose this alternative—perhaps sensing his impending downfall, he says only that "it appears to be this way" (342b8)—but he really has no choice, having himself stressed and championed the flawlessness of the arts.

Thrasymachus' "choice" here is dictated, however, not only by his commitment to painting the arts in the best possible light, but also by his apparent acceptance of Socrates' articulation of the alternatives. Yet are Socrates' three alternatives truly exhaustive? And is any one of them, especially the one Socrates gets Thrasymachus to choose, in fact a correct presentation of the arts? To begin with, we should note that in all three alternatives, every art is portrayed as being on the same level as every other art, as either equally defective or equally perfect. As Socrates presents it, either *all* arts are defective—either *all* such that each needs another art to remedy its defects, or *all* such that each is able to remedy its own defects—or *no* arts are defective at all. Socrates leaves out the possibility of a hierarchy of arts, a hierarchy in which some superior arts direct and thus complete other, inferior arts and at the peak of which might even be a single art, or, perhaps better to say, a single form of knowledge, ultimately directing all the arts.[20] The need, however, for such a hierarchical understanding would seem to be suggested not only by the existence of hierarchies within various spheres of arts (e.g., shipbuilding is subordinate to piloting) but also by the fact that each of the arts, or spheres of arts, is directed to and serves only some particular human need. Only a form of knowledge higher than the arts (or higher than the *other* arts, if one wishes to call it too an art), namely, knowledge of the good, would be able to relate these particular needs to the complete human good.[21]

Now, Socrates' present account of the arts and knowledge avoids mentioning or even pointing to the need for such knowledge. But this may require a certain distortion concerning the ultimate ends of the arts. Socrates describes the arts as arising out of needs and as directed to serving needs. Yet the particular needs that Socrates mentions are never related in his account to the complete good of complete human beings. Socrates speaks, in the first place, of the needs of parts of human beings—bodies, eyes, and ears (341e2–7, 342a2–4)—without speaking of the needs of full human beings, or even of human beings as such (contrast 341c6, c9). The difficulty with leaving it at this, however, becomes clearer in Socrates' next examples in which he repeats his usual example of medicine but now places alongside it, in the position previously occupied by piloting, the example of horsemanship (342c1–4; cf. 341c4–10 as well as 342d3–10). Socrates claims that horsemanship serves the needs of horses,

20. Compare Aristotle, *Nicomachean Ethics* 1094a6–27; see also Benardete, p. 24.

21. See again Bloom, p. 322: "The doctor can produce health, but that health is good he does not learn from medicine, and similarly with all the other arts. . . . To help a sick friend one needs not only a doctor but someone who knows to whom health is fitting and how many other goods should be sacrificed to it and who can direct the doctor to do what will most help the patient." See also Averroes, pp. 86–88.

that it is directed to the advantage of horses. But does it really make sense to maintain that horses are the final end of horsemanship? Horsemen train horses, one would ultimately have to admit, not for the sake of the horses themselves but in order to serve higher arts, like generalship and farming, which are more clearly and directly pursued for the sake of human ends.[22] And these human ends, in turn—ends like victory in war and bodily nourishment—must ultimately be related to one another and placed within a hierarchy of ends ordered by reference to the human good. To admit this, though, is to admit that the arts are not as perfect as Socrates here presents them, to grant that they call for guidance by a higher kind of knowledge that knows the human good.

But why would Socrates want to avoid this? To get an idea, first let us look at the conclusion Socrates draws from Thrasymachus' choice of the alternative by which the arts are perfect. Having gotten Thrasymachus to agree to the perfection of the arts, Socrates has secured the basis for the arts' unconcern with their own advantage. No art, he argues, looks to its own good, for no art needs to. Each art looks instead to the good of that of which it is an art, which is defective and needs the art (342c1–6). From here the path to Thrasymachus' defeat is clear. For Socrates is now able to use Thrasymachus' own analogy between art and rule—both the aspect by which art is a form of rule, inasmuch as each art rules over that of which it is an art, as well as the aspect by which rule is like the arts, inasmuch as it is a form of knowledge (see 340e4–6)—to insist on the directedness of all rule and all knowledge to the advantage of the weaker and the ruled (342c8–d1). Finally, taking advantage of the assumption that what is true of the arts and rule must be true also of the artisans and rulers, and recalling Thrasymachus' earlier agreement about the character of the true doctor and the true pilot (342d3–e5), Socrates draws this conclusion:

> No one in any position of rule, insofar as he is ruling, looks after or commands his own advantage, but rather [he looks after and commands] the advantage of that which is ruled, that of which he himself is a craftsman. Looking to this,

---

22. See Aristotle, *Nicomachean Ethics* 1094a6–16.

and what is advantageous and fitting for it, he says everything he says and does everything he does. (342e6–11)

This conclusion completes Socrates' argument, and it seems also
to complete his victory over Thrasymachus. Having reached this
point, Socrates says that it was clear to everyone present that
Thrasymachus' definition of justice, or, literally, his "speech about
justice," had been stood on its head (343a1–2). By Socrates' argument, to which Thrasymachus has been compelled to assent, justice
appears to reside not in the weak's obedience to the self-serving laws
and commands of the strong but in the service the strong selflessly
perform for the weak. Far from exploiting the ruled, true rulers take
care of the ruled like doctors taking care of patients. By using
Thrasymachus' commitment to knowledge and the arts, Socrates
seems finally to have addressed and refuted Thrasymachus' fundamental claim about justice, for he has shown that those rulers who
are knowers, those rulers whom Thrasymachus admires most, are
not guided by their own good but rule for the sake of the ruled.

Yet the difficulty we have touched on remains. Socrates has gotten Thrasymachus to agree to an inadequate account of the arts, one
that abstracts, to repeat, from the deficiencies in the arts, and in particular from the arts' ultimate subordinacy to knowledge of the
human good. Does Socrates' refutation of Thrasymachus rest on this
abstraction? Is Socrates able, in other words, to assert the directedness of all knowledge (and so of rule insofar as it is conceived of as a
form of knowledge) to the good of something other than its possessor only by limiting the knowledge he is talking about—that is, by
not in fact talking about *all* knowledge (cf. 342c11–d1)?

To see the difficulty more clearly we must consider the case of a
possessor of knowledge not of some particular art but of what is
good for human beings as complete beings, of the human good. For
while it might be plausible to maintain that artisans, at least when
viewed strictly and solely in their role *as artisans*,[23] possess a knowledge that is directed to meeting some need or serving some end other

---

23. Another question one could raise about Socrates' account of the arts is
whether it makes sense to assume that if the *arts* themselves are selfless then the *artisans* are too. The basis of the arts' selflessness, as Socrates here presents it, is their

than their own good—e.g., that the doctor's knowledge of the medical art is directed to healing sick bodies—it is more doubtful that the knowledge possessed by someone who knows the human good could be disinterested in the same way. Such a man's knowledge would necessarily pertain to his own case as well as to the cases of any others he might want to help. Unlike the doctor who is only occasionally and accidentally sick, and so only occasionally and accidentally the object of his own knowledge, the man who knows the human good is always and necessarily a human being with concern for his own human well-being. In fact, the need for and drive toward knowledge of the human good would seem to arise above all out of the insufficiency of other knowledge, including that of the arts, to provide adequately for *one's own* good (see 505a2–b3, d5–e1; see also Aristotle, *Nicomachean Ethics* 1094a22–24). This means, though, that Socrates cannot ultimately base a true argument for the selflessness of knowers as such, and hence of rulers understood as knowers, simply on the selflessness of knowledge, for knowledge in its highest form is not selfless. Indeed, it turns out that we have seen only a provisional and preliminary account of the selfless artisan-knower-ruler.

Thrasymachus' Attack on Justice: The Shepherd Speech and Its Aftermath (343a2–347e4)

Socrates will return to reconsider the arts. What prompts him to do so, however, is an extended speech by Thrasymachus, which we need to look at next. Thrasymachus' speech is first of all an expression of his frustration with Socrates' preceding argument. Although Thrasymachus has been unable to escape the movement of Socrates' argument to the conclusion that artisans and rulers look to the good only of the ruled, this obviously does not mean that he has been persuaded or convinced. Yet, if we look at the character of Thrasymachus' frustration, we see that Thrasymachus has been convinced of at least something: he is convinced that *Socrates believes* what he has argued.

---

self-sufficiency. Artisans, however, when viewed not only as vehicles of knowledge but as human beings, have needs and concerns that their arts do not. Socrates will acknowledge the importance of this difference in his reconsideration of the arts later in Book One.

Whereas Thrasymachus had earlier accused Socrates of being a syco-phant—someone, that is, who cleverly exploits justice for his own gain—he now compares Socrates to a child with a runny nose (343a3–8).[24] Exasperated by the amazing naiveté of Socrates' appar-ent belief in selfless artisan-rulers, Thrasymachus delivers not only a biting criticism of Socrates but also his most explicit and radical attack on the goodness of justice (his speech runs from 343b1–344c8, with 343a7–9 as an introduction).

Thrasymachus begins with a simple objection to Socrates' por-trayal of the arts. Socrates, he says, does not even understand shep-herds and sheep (343a8–9). Misled by the shepherd's concern for his flock, his care to watch over and fatten his sheep, Socrates fails to see that the sheep are hardly the final objects of this concern. Aren't the sheep, after all, destined to be eaten or at least shorn? Any concern for the sheep, as everyone knows but some forget, is guided and cir-cumscribed by the shepherd's concern for his master and for himself (343b1–4).

Now, Thrasymachus does acknowledge here that the shepherd must take *some* care of his sheep; the shepherd must look to the good of his sheep *to some extent*. Moreover, Thrasymachus' mention of the shepherd's master is a (perhaps unwitting) admission that the good of some human beings may depend in certain circumstances on serving the good of others.[25] Yet the best way to overcome this prob-lem, one might think, is to become the master oneself. And indeed it is not shepherds but rulers whom Thrasymachus has most in mind. The shepherd example only paves the way for Thrasymachus' return to rulers. Just as Socrates does not understand the true disposition of shepherds toward sheep, Thrasymachus declares, Socrates does not see that rulers "in the cities," at least those who know what they are doing, those "truly ruling," look on the ruled no less as objects of exploitation: "you [Socrates] believe that [rulers] regard the ruled somehow differently than a man regards sheep, and that night and day they consider anything other than this: whence they themselves will benefit" (343b4–c1).

---

24. Compare 343a3–8 with 340d1, 341a5–c3 as well as 336c2–6, 337a3–7, e1–3, 338b1–3.

25. See Strauss, *The City and Man*, pp. 81–82; Benardete, p. 26.

Thrasymachus' statement here about rulers, prepared by the analogy of shepherds, is itself only a prelude to his most massive attack on what he takes to be Socrates' understanding of justice and on justice itself: "And you [Socrates] are so far off concerning the just and justice, and the unjust and injustice, that you do not know that justice and the just are, in truth, the good of another" (343c1–4). Justice, Thrasymachus asserts, is essentially serving others. Now, if we pause for a moment at this point in his speech, we may be surprised by the thought that despite his rebuke of Socrates, what Thrasymachus says here about justice seems remarkably similar to what Socrates has been saying about the arts, that they are selfless and directed to the good of others. In fact, to say that justice is the good of another could seem, at face value, to be a *praise* of justice; from a certain perspective, one which Socrates' depiction of the arts evokes, the thought that justice involves devotion to the good of another is precisely what makes justice so admirable and impressive.[26] Yet aside from noting that Thrasymachus, unlike Socrates, claims that it is the weak who serve the strong (343c4, cf., however, d3–e7), we can wonder whether those who see the concern with the good of another as what elevates rather than demotes justice would be willing to take Thrasymachus' next step. By serving others, Thrasymachus says, the just man harms himself.[27] This is Thrasymachus' full statement:

> . . . justice is the good of another, the advantage of the one who is stronger and rules, *but a personal harm to the one who obeys and serves*; injustice is the opposite, and it rules the truly simple and just. Those who are ruled serve the advantage of the one who is stronger, and by serving him, they make him happy *but themselves not at all*." (343c3–d1, emphasis added).

As many commentators have stressed, this statement is a crucial turning point in the conversation between Thrasymachus and Socra-

---

26. Compare Aristotle, *Nicomachean Ethics* 1129b25–1130a13.
27. Contrast Aristotle, *Nicomachean Ethics* 1136b20–22, or Plato, *Laws* 662c5–663c8 and context.

tes, and even in the *Republic* as a whole.[28] Thrasymachus makes explicit here his attack on justice, saying outright what he had left implicit up to this point, namely, that there is no common good and that being just, serving others, is bad for the just man himself. Thrasymachus thus goes further in his present speech than he has in any of his earlier statements. This increased radicalism must be understood, however, in light of at least one qualification: especially since Thrasymachus is attacking justice, we must first make sure we know simply what justice is according to his present speech. Just to review briefly his earlier statements on this point, Thrasymachus began by arguing that justice consists in nothing more than obedience to the laws set down by the ruling group in each city (338d7–339a4); but then he modified this position—so I argued—with his later statement on rulers in the strict sense, a statement that was more paradoxical and less clear about what justice is than his initial statement (340c6–341a4; see pp. 70–71 above). Now, if he did in fact modify his position, the first thing we can say about Thrasymachus' present speech is that he seems here to be moving back to the more commonsensical understanding of justice from which he began.[29] But it is not enough to say this, for what Thrasymachus says in his pre-

---

28. See, for example, Annas, *An Introduction*, p. 45; Sallis, p. 341; Nickolas Pappas, *Plato and the Republic* (London: Routledge, 1995), p. 44; Bloom, pp. 334–335; Darrell Dobbs, "Choosing Justice: Socrates' Model City and the Practice of Dialectic," *American Political Science Review* 88 (1994): 263–277, p. 263; Irwin, *Plato's Ethics*, p. 176.

29. One must consider all of 343b4–344c2. The only remnant of Thrasymachus' "strict sense" speech is the phrase "those truly ruling" at 343b4, but even this should be read in light of the preceding "in the cities." Much of the scholarship on the Thrasymachus section of the *Republic* centers around the question of whether Thrasymachus sticks to a consistent understanding of justice throughout his conversation with Socrates. The main issue that prompts the debate is whether the statement at 343c4–5, that justice is the good of another, should be taken as a definition of justice, and if so, whether this can be squared with the earlier definition of justice as the advantage of the stronger. My own view, expressed in the present paragraph in the text, should be contrasted with both of the two main sides of the debate, for I suggest neither that Thrasymachus *defines* justice as the good of another nor that he is simply consistent. Allowing for some differences in their readings, proponents of the view that Thrasymachus shifts to a new definition of justice as the good of another are Cross and Woozely, pp. 38–41; Macquire, pp. 147–151; and Sparshott, pp. 428–434. Roughly on this side are also Sallis, p. 341; Annas, *An Introduction*, pp. 45–46; and Kerferd, "The Doctrine of Thrasymachus," pp. 19–27, "Thrasy-

sent speech is not simply identical even to his opening statement, which was a very radical or unconventional statement in its own right. In a certain respect, what Thrasymachus says now is *more* in line with the common, ordinary view of justice. For one thing, Thrasymachus has just spoken of some rulers as unjust, and he will go on in his speech to admit the possibility of just rulers as well (343c5–7, e1–7, see also 344a2–c6); earlier, the rulers were said to be the source of justice and therefore it was strictly speaking impossible to speak of the rulers' own justice or injustice (see pp. 63–65 above). In his present speech, Thrasymachus broadens the range of justice: it exists beyond the purview of the laws of any given city and means more than obedience to such laws (see especially 343d3–344c2). He broadens justice to mean something like fairness and concern for others; to be just, we can say, is the opposite of *pleonektein*, to take advantage of others and grab more than one's fair share.[30]

Of course, even if he has in mind a broader, more ordinary understanding of what justice is, Thrasymachus is attacking justice so understood, arguing not that it is not justice but that one is a fool to be just. In this most important respect Thrasymachus' speech remains his most radical moment thus far. And intending not merely to assert the inferiority of justice, Thrasymachus devotes the next part of his speech to providing evidence for his argument: "One must consider, most simple Socrates, that the just man everywhere has less than the unjust man" (343d1–3).

Thrasymachus outlines three situations in which the just man fares worse than the unjust man (343d3–e6). First, in contracts, when a just man and an unjust man form and then later dissolve a partnership, the just man, according to Thrasymachus, always ends up with less than his unjust partner. So too in the affairs of the city, taxes and distributions, the just man always comes out behind, giving more and taking less. Finally, when the just man gets a chance to

---

machus and Justice," pp. 12–16. Dissenters who argue (albeit in different ways) that Thrasymachus adheres more or less consistently to his original presentation at 338c1–339a4 are Reeve, pp. 16–19, 270, n. 13; Lycos, p. 56; Hourani, pp. 110–120; and Henderson, pp. 218–228.

30. The term *pleonektein*, which will play a large role from here on, is introduced at 343d5–6 and 344a1. Compare Aristotle, *Nicomachean Ethics* 1129a31–b10.

rule, even if nothing else goes wrong, he must watch his private affairs deteriorate from neglect and his family and friends come to despise him, all because he is unwilling to help either himself or them more than would be just. In each of these examples, Thrasymachus sees that justice is a restraint on the just man, and accordingly he draws the conclusion that the goods that justice restrains the just man from freely pursuing, the goods that Thrasymachus claims make one happy, can more easily be gotten if one disregards this restraint and turns to injustice. Whereas the just man suffers in each of the examples, for the unjust man "everything is reversed" (343e7).

Yet Thrasymachus seems to have ignored here an obvious difficulty in his case: there are obstacles standing in the way of injustice too. Justice, after all, is not merely an internal restraint; it is also enforced by the harsh punishments and reproaches that are almost everywhere inflicted on those who commit injustices, at least when they are caught.[31] Thrasymachus acknowledges this difficulty as he continues (see 344b1–5). In fact, this may explain why he moves next and for the rest of his speech to the case of "the most complete injustice," that is, to that form of injustice that is so thoroughly successful that it overcomes the problems that ordinarily plague injustice and thus leaves the one who commits it "most happy" (344a3–5). Thrasymachus tells Socrates to consider tyranny, for the tyrant not only seizes the goods of others by deception and by force but he also escapes punishment since he enslaves the people themselves (344a6–b6). Nor does the tyrant, according to Thrasymachus, even suffer reproach: whereas those who commit ordinary, small-scale injustices are called by shameful names—temple robbers, kidnappers, housebreakers, cheaters, and thieves—the tyrant is called happy and blessed "not only by the citizens but by everyone else who hears that he has committed the whole of injustice" (344b1–c2).

Once again, however, Thrasymachus seems to have overestimated the ease of his case: Is it really true that tyrants are not reproached? Even Thrasymachus himself seems to admit, as he continues, that it is not simply true, that in fact people reproach *all* injustice, including tyranny (see 344c3–4). But Thrasymachus thinks he

---

31. See the objection of the Just Speech to the Unjust Speech in Aristophanes' *Clouds*, 1083–1084 and context.

can explain these reproaches such that they are not inconsistent with an admiration of tyranny. Those who reproach injustice, he argues, do so not because they fear committing injustice—not, that is, because they are genuinely attached to justice—but because they fear suffering injustice (344c3–4). Whatever they may say with their mouths, in other words, those who reproach injustice are in their hearts no more just than anyone else; even their "just speeches" can be traced to a selfish or unjust motive. Thrasymachus thinks, then, that he can still maintain that his defense of injustice is simply an articulation of a universal, if frequently hidden, belief that successful injustice makes the man who commits it happy.

But there is at least one difficulty here. Just moments earlier in this same speech, Thrasymachus painted a much different picture of the just man. He portrayed him as naively taken in by justice, as genuinely devoted to serving others, and genuinely respectful of the limits justice sets (see 343c6–7, d3–e6, 344a6). In fact, Thrasymachus said as much about Socrates himself, reversing his original opinion that Socrates is a sycophant in light of Socrates' apparent belief in his argument on behalf of justice (see pp. 78–79 above and 343d2). When we try to put these earlier statements together with what he says now, Thrasymachus appears less certain that there is never such a thing as sincere respect for justice; he appears confused or unsure as to whether anyone is ever truly just.

Something else, too, is puzzling about Thrasymachus' statement regarding the base motive underlying the reproaches of injustice. Thrasymachus tries to uncover this motive because he wants to show the disingenuousness of these reproaches. He wants to expose their hypocrisy. But simply as a matter of prudence—or, in other words, on Thrasymachus' own grounds—aren't these reproaches smart? Aren't those who reproach injustice, we can even ask, acting much more prudently than Thrasymachus himself is acting by openly attacking justice in his present speech? To answer this question it is not essential to know whether these reproaches are in fact merely prudential (as opposed to sincerely believed) but only to consider whether they do not make good sense if one looks at them as such. Indeed, particularly if one fully adopts Thrasymachus' own perspective—there is no common good, the just serve the unjust, and tyranny is best—prudence would seem to counsel that one praise justice and reproach injustice, or at a minimum that one remain silent, for by doing the opposite one encourages others to become one's masters or at least one's rivals.[32]

Given Thrasymachus' failure to take this prudent course, the question arises of why Thrasymachus so openly attacks justice. What explains his openness, especially if it is imprudent? And this puzzle may lead us to a surprising possibility: Could it be that Thrasymachus' vehement attack on justice, his seemingly most unjust moment, is the very thing that gives the strongest indication that he is more attached to justice, more just, than perhaps even he himself ever thought? To spell this out, is it not possible that Thrasymachus' zeal to expose the harmfulness of justice to the just can be explained, at least in part, as the product of indignation at the (perceived) fact that justice leads to the suffering of the just and an accompanying desire to keep others from being duped by justice?[33] Against this suggestion, one might say that Thrasymachus' attack on justice is not so imprudent and can be explained by simpler and more selfish motives: he wants the prestige and perhaps also the money and followers that displaying his knowledge will bring him.[34] But to see that there may be more to it than simple self-interest, we should recall that Thrasymachus was angry at Socrates earlier in the discussion for concealing his wisdom about justice.[35] He was angry at Socrates, in other words,

---

32. Henderson approaches the same point from a slightly different angle: "It is interesting to note in passing that Thrasymachus might well have argued that Socrates, who is known for his attempts to defend the just life as the best and most profitable life for man, is actually playing into the hands of the unjust ruler. [A prudent tyrant] would want everyone in the state (except himself who knows better) to act justly, to live just lives, and to believe sincerely that in doing so they were serving their own best interests" (pp. 222–223).

33. See p. 68 and note 12 above. Also compare *Gorgias* 511b1–6, which should be read not only in its immediate context but in light of Callicles' preceding attack on justice. If my suggestion here about Thrasymachus is correct, his indignation is tantamount to blaming justice for being unjust, or fairness for being unfair— in other words, he is both still attached to justice and confused. Consider also Friedländer's remark (paraphrasing Thrasymachus' view), "with reference to the tyrant, it makes no sense to speak of crimes" (p. 63); yet Thrasymachus *does* speak of the tyrant as a criminal. On this last point, see also Reeve, pp. 18–19.

34. See Nichols, p. 51; Howland, pp. 71–72, 74–75.

35. See again 336c2–d4, 337a3–7, e1–3, 338b1–3. In this early part of the conversation, Thrasymachus seemed to think that Socrates in fact possessed wisdom about justice; he may even have thought that Socrates held the same view of justice that he expressed: consider 338c2–3 where Thrasymachus seemed to expect that

for not showing the candor he shows, and this suggests—if we follow an earlier suggestion of Socrates that anger betrays an uncertainty that the course of action one opposes is really so foolish[36]—that Thrasymachus must have some doubts that his own openness is really in his own best interests. Even if we update Thrasymachus' view and say that he no longer regards Socrates as someone who conceals his wisdom but rather as a naive innocent, we then have to ask why such naiveté would so manifestly bother Thrasymachus and prompt him to seek to corrupt it (see again especially 343a2–d3; see note 12). For some reason, Thrasymachus is not content to leave the innocents to their innocence—an innocence that makes them so much easier to exploit—as a simply cold-blooded unjust man would be.

Nevertheless, whatever confusions or lingering attachments may be driving Thrasymachus, we must not lose sight of the explicit, face-value significance of his speech. Thrasymachus ends his speech with a summary, proclaiming that injustice, when it is committed on a sufficient scale, is "stronger, freer, and more masterful" than justice, and that it is the unjust man who truly profits himself and serves his own advantage (344c4–8). Perhaps for reasons we have just considered, perhaps, that is, because he begins to realize his imprudence, Thrasymachus wants to leave after he has finished his speech (344d1–3). But the audience will not let him go (344d4–5). Even Socrates himself urges Thrasymachus to stay:

> Daimonic Thrasymachus, having thrown in such a speech, do you intend to leave before teaching us sufficiently or learning whether [what you have claimed] is true or not? Or do you think you are trying to determine a small matter instead of the way of life[37] by which each of us would live the most profitable life? (344d6–e3)

Socrates' response to his definition of justice would be one of mere public disapproval not true disagreement.

36. Consider the implications of 336e2–337a2. See also note 37 to chapter 1 above.

37. I am following manuscripts A, D, and M, which have *all' ou biou* at 344e1–2, rather than *holou biou* as Burnet takes it following manuscript F. As Burnet has it, the text could be translated: "Or do you think that it is a small matter to determine the way of [one's] whole life . . ." See Adam, p. 41; Allen, p. 102. Consider 344e4–7.

With these questions, Socrates highlights and appears to accept an important result of Thrasymachus' speech: the topic under discussion has now shifted from the question of what justice is, to the question of what the most profitable life is, and more narrowly, to the question of whether this life is the just or the unjust one (see also 344e5–345b3). Against Thrasymachus' claim that the unjust life is the happiest, Socrates will give a defense of the goodness of justice for the just.

Before he does so, however, Socrates has a last set of arguments to make against Thrasymachus' portrayal of artisans and rulers and the understanding of justice that accords with that portrayal. To clarify, then, the somewhat complicated crossroads we have come to in the discussion: although Socrates stresses the shift to the question of the goodness of justice, and although he acknowledges the importance of this question, he now postpones taking up this question in order to return to an earlier topic; as he himself puts it, he backtracks so that he and Thrasymachus may further consider "the previous things" (345b8–c1).

These "previous things" are in the first place the arts, and Socrates begins by faulting Thrasymachus for not sticking to the view of the arts that had been arrived at prior to Thrasymachus' speech. Against Thrasymachus' portrayal in particular of the shepherd's art as directed to the good of the shepherd rather than the sheep, Socrates reasserts the view that every art, every form of rule, looks not to its own good but to the good of the ruled (345c1–e2). The basis of this other-directedness of the arts is the same as it was before: since the arts, inasmuch as they are fully arts, are already perfect, they are not needy (345d1–5; see again 342b1–c6 and pp. 74, 76 above). Socrates appears, then, simply to be revisiting and trying to reestablish his earlier argument about the arts, and to be resting this argument on the same understanding of the arts that we found questionable before (see pp. 74–77 above). Yet with Socrates' next question a difference and perhaps an improvement begins to make itself felt. Turning from the other arts to rule in the more narrow and usual sense, that is, political rule, Socrates asks Thrasymachus whether he thinks those who rule in the cities, those who truly rule, do so voluntarily (345e2–3).

After an emphatic reply from Thrasymachus—"By Zeus, I don't only think that, I know it well" (345e4)—Socrates does not respond directly. Instead, having just turned to political rule, he turns just as quickly back to "the other forms of rule," to the other arts (345e5). Doesn't Thrasymachus know, he asks, that none of the other artisans practices his art voluntarily, but that each requires an incentive external to his art itself to induce him to practice his art (345e5–6)? This incentive is the wage the artisan receives for practicing his art, and Socrates here outlines the so-called "wage-earning art" that each artisan must possess in addition to his own specific art in order to be willing to practice that art.

Socrates offers the following account of the arts and their relationship to wage-earning (346a1–d8). Each of the arts, he gets Thrasymachus to agree, can be distinguished from the other arts by its specific capacity (*dunamis*). Corresponding to its specific capacity, moreover, each art provides "us" (346a6) with a specific benefit, a benefit that, because it corresponds to that art's specific capacity, is the province of that art alone. Thus, to give one of Socrates' examples, health is the benefit corresponding to the capacity of the medical art, hence it is the province of that art alone. Even if one were to produce health while practicing another art (by breathing fresh air while sailing for instance) that other art should not be equated or confused with medicine, for that other art produces health only as an accidental by-product, not as the benefit corresponding to its specific capacity (safety on the sea rather than health is the benefit specific to sailing). The purpose of this "precise distinguishing" (346b3) is not only to keep the many different arts distinct from one another, but especially to keep all the other arts, each of which might seem to procure wages for the artisan, distinct from wage-earning. As Socrates presents it here, each artisan should be understood as practicing two distinct arts, the specific one for which he is known (e.g., the doctor practices medicine) and the wage-earning art that is common to all artisans. The benefit for the artisan himself comes from his practice of the latter art, the wage-earning art.

Understanding the ubiquitous wage-earning art in this way allows Socrates to preserve the directedness of the other arts to the good of objects other than the artisan himself. At a certain point (346e3–4), Socrates stops referring to wage-earning as an art, but still preserves its importance; he is thereby able to present this conclusion:

Thus, Thrasymachus, it is clear by now that none of the arts, nor any of the forms of rule, procures its own benefit, but rather, just as we have been saying for a long time, each procures and commands [the benefit of] the ruled; it considers the advantage of that one, the advantage of the weaker, not the stronger. (346e3–7)

Socrates reaches the same conclusion about the arts, in other words, that he had reached earlier (see 341c4–342e1). But whereas this had appeared as great praise of the arts before, it is now said to be the reason the arts are deficient:

This, Thrasymachus my friend, is why I said just a moment ago that no one chooses voluntarily to rule and to make it his task to straighten out the troubles of others, but instead [every artisan-ruler] demands wages. (346e7–347a1)

We must try to draw out the significance of "wage-earning" and the change it represents from Socrates' earlier account of the arts. To begin with, we should notice that Socrates' portrayal of the arts in this section invites us to consider the arts as forming a kind of community: each art provides "us" (346a6) with some benefit or addresses some need.[38] To spell this out a bit, we may say that the arts, or the artisans, seem to be the parts of an interdependent whole, a whole to which each contributes as an artisan and through which everyone's needs are met by the services of others. In the later books of the *Republic*, the division of labor and specialization, each person performing his or her own specific task for the sake of the whole, will even be the principle of justice in Socrates' ideal city (see especially 433a1–444c10). Yet here in the present section, Socrates focuses our attention on the *basis* of each artisan's participation in such a whole or community, and in particular on what leads each artisan to make his own contribution. It is in making his own contribution, practicing his own specific art, that each artisan devotes himself to others or to the common good. And yet he does so, according to Socrates' present account, neither out of an intrinsic love of practicing his art nor out of true devotion to the good of those he serves. Since the practice of each art requires that the artisan direct a great deal of his energy to addressing what is only one of the many particular human needs, and that he spend a

---

38. See Bloom's note 41, pp. 445–446.

great deal of his time serving others, it is understandable that each artisan is not drawn to his art as something intrinsically satisfying or good for him. *Indirectly*, of course, an artisan's art can become attractive and good for him if he receives wages (with which he can then in turn purchase the services of the other artisans); but this only underlines the deficiency of the practice of the art itself, as distinct from wage-earning. The necessity, that is, that wage-earning accompany each of the arts is a reflection of the inadequacy of the arts—precisely if they are understood as other-directed and distinct from wage-earning—from the perspective of the artisan's own good (see 347a1–3).[39] Moreover, the necessity of wages is also a reflection of the supreme importance of that perspective. For if wage-earning is that which makes the artisans willing to practice the arts, wage-earning would seem to have a kind of sovereignty over the arts. And what that means in terms of the artisan, who is portrayed as both a servant of others (through his particular art) and a wage-earner for himself, is that what "wage-earning" stands for—his concern for his own good—is more fundamental than what the arts demand. As Socrates presents it here, it is ultimately for the sake of his own private good, and only because that good must sometimes be served by indirect means, that each artisan "devotes" himself to others or contributes to the community.[40]

Now—just to take this one step further—given that his own good is of fundamental importance to the artisan, knowledge of that good would be most valuable to him. Such knowledge does not, of course, belong to him as an artisan, for as Socrates stresses, each artisan's particular art knows how to address only some particular or partial need. Nor does it even belong to a community of artisans taken as a whole, for as we noted earlier, since each of the arts serves only a particular need, the arts may point toward but not yet possess, not even all of them together, the higher, trans-technical knowledge

---

39. Compare Aristotle, *Nicomachean Ethics* 1134b1–7; contrast Schleiermacher, p. 375.

40. Compare Nichols, pp. 51–52: ". . . one of the consequences of the selflessness of art [is that] artisans must be paid for their services. It is precisely because they serve others rather than themselves through their arts that they must be given wages for practicing their arts. Socrates thus concedes to Thrasymachus that men are selfish even while maintaining the selflessness of art." See also Sallis, p. 340; Reeve, p. 19; Bloom, pp. 332–334. Strauss, *The City and Man*, p. 81, writes: ". . . the essentially just arts are ultimately in the service of an art which is not essentially just. Thrasymachus' view, according to which the private good is supreme, triumphs."

that could order their various ends and orient them toward the complete human good (see pp. 75–76 above). What the present discussion adds, though, to the earlier account of the arts is an implicit recognition of the importance of such knowledge not only to guide the arts but for the sake of the artisan himself as an individual.

Perhaps connected with this, we should notice that Socrates vacillates in this section between calling and not calling wage-earning an art (see 345e5–346a1 then 346b1–d6 then 346d6–347a6). Why does he do so? On the one hand, Socrates does not want to call wage-earning an art because he wants to maintain that the arts as such are other-directed (see 346e3–7). On the other hand, he may want to call wage-earning an art at least in some places in order to get us to think about the possibility that what wage-earning stands for can be a matter of *knowledge*, that is, to keep us from assuming that knowledge can be found only in the various particular arts and that mere greed, desire, and opinion must provide any further guidance. In other words, if the necessity of wage-earning bespeaks the fundamental importance of one's own good, calling it the "art" of wage-earning may point to the importance and possibility of knowledge of one's own good, a knowledge that would have to be based, presumably, on knowledge of the human good as such.

It is fitting, then, that Socrates goes on in the next turn in the conversation to speak of a group of men who seem to be possessors of such knowledge. He speaks in particular of how they would be disposed toward ruling. The question of ruling resurfaces when Socrates brings the argument about the arts back to rule, that is, back to political rule understood as an art. Using the conclusion already reached about the arts, Socrates argues that since the art of ruling, as an art, serves not the ruler but the ruled, no one would voluntarily rule unless a wage were attached, either money or honor or a penalty if one should not rule (347a3–6). It is not clear why ruling could not be understood on the model of wage-earning rather than the other arts—as the wage-seizing art, or something along such lines. But rather than having to respond to any such objection from Thrasymachus, Socrates gets a question from Glaucon. Glaucon interrupts because he does not understand the third "wage" Socrates speaks of, the penalty if one should not rule. What penalty is Socrates referring to and what does it mean to classify it as a wage (347a7–9)? In response to this question, Socrates gives an extended statement about how ruling is regarded by "the best" men (347a10), or "the most decent" (347b1), or "the good" (347b6). The term Socrates uses to refer to the group in question varies (see also 347c6 and d2–3); perhaps the most revealing formulation is the final one: "everyone who knows" (347d6).

Socrates says that in not understanding the third wage, the penalty, Glaucon fails to understand the only wage that can ever induce the best men to rule (347a10–b1). Since they desire neither money nor honor,[41] such men would be willing to rule only when there is some penalty attached to not ruling. The greatest and most compelling penalty, according to Socrates, is to be ruled by a worse man if they themselves are unwilling to rule (347b1–c5). Now, we should notice that Socrates' statement seems to begin here from a certain kind of high-mindedness that is probably admired by Glaucon, a high-mindedness that looks down with disdain on the greedy or vain pursuit of money or honor and approaches rule with the reluctance of a kind of noblesse oblige (see 347b1–4 and c2–3 in particular; cf. 489b6–c3). This lofty tone, moreover, seems to fit well with Socrates' present and final dismissal of Thrasymachus' argument that rule serves the advantage of the rulers and that, in this sense, justice is the advantage of the stronger (347d4–6, d8–e1). Yet we need to look more closely at the character of the best men's attitude toward rule. For as his statement progresses, Socrates makes it increasingly clear that the basis of his contention that rule does not serve the rulers' own advantage is not ultimately that true rulers— any more than the other artisans—nobly transcend a concern for their own good, but only that when viewed from the highest perspective, rule appears to offer only labor and toil but no true positive goods (347c5–d2). To illustrate the attitude of the best toward rule, Socrates imagines a hypothetical city populated only by good men (347d2–4). In such a city, he suggests, the citizens could not even be drawn to rule by the "wage" of avoiding being ruled by a worse man, and although it would still be necessary for someone to rule (if only

---

41. The case of money is not so clear. What Socrates literally says is that good men are unwilling to rule for the sake of money because they want to avoid the reputation of being either hirelings or thieves. This is odd because it seem to grant that good men regard money as a good, something Socrates denies in the case of honor, but as a good subordinate to reputation (which, curiously, is at least akin to honor).

to keep order) nobody would want to be the one to bear that burden. As Socrates strikingly sums it up: "everyone who knows would prefer to be benefited by another rather than to take upon himself the troubles of benefiting others" (347d6–8).[42] Socrates' disagreement with Thrasymachus, it seems, and the basis of his present rejection of Thrasymachus' definition of justice as the advantage of the stronger (contrast with 342e6–343a2), is not finally about whether rulers and knowers are concerned first and foremost with their own good, but only about what the true human good is and what activities knowledge of it leads one to pursue. Socrates does not identify here what he and "everyone who knows" regard as the true human good, but while knowledge of it, judging by his indications, does not encourage a great concern with money or honor, neither does it make one eager to undertake the burdens of rule or to benefit others more generally. The attitude of "everyone who knows" to these latter "goods" is of particular significance, furthermore, for at least in a certain respect it reveals their attitude toward justice itself: ruling for the sake of the ruled and benefiting others are ordinarily taken to be preeminent examples of justice, not to say its very meaning. Socrates' present statement about rule thus leads to the suggestion that "everyone who knows" regards justice as something that is sometimes, perhaps even frequently, good for them, but never in more than a limited sense. It is good in the way in which a necessary evil is good. Given certain circumstances, that is to say, it is needed and its absence would be worse than its presence; in the best imaginable case, however, circumstances would be such that one could do without it. To put this another way, Socrates suggests here that justice is not in itself desirable for an individual but that it relies on the ills of defective situations to give it what true necessity and "goodness" it can possess.[43]

It is somewhat surprising, to be sure, that such a conclusion should be one of the results of what Socrates says is his final attempt to explain why he disagrees with Thrasymachus' definition of justice.

---

42. Compare 496c5–e2, 499b3–6, 500b8–c7, 517c7–b2, 519b7–d7, 540a4–c2; but cf. 497a3–5. Compare also Aristotle, *Politics* 1279a10–13.
43. See Strauss, *The City and Man*, pp. 82–83.

Yet, in examining as closely as we have Socrates' remarks about rule, perhaps we have overstepped a line that Socrates wishes to draw between the question of what justice is and the question of whether justice is good. At any rate, Socrates suggests after finishing his statement on rule that *only now* will he turn from the question of whether justice is the advantage of the stronger to Thrasymachus' "much greater" claim that "the unjust life is superior to the just life" (347e2–4). That is, Socrates reminds us at this point, or urges us to think, that while Thrasymachus' long speech, his "shepherd speech"—with the attack it advanced against the goodness of justice—initiated a transition in the discussion, this transition is not yet complete, since Socrates himself has yet to turn his attention from the question, "What is justice?" to the question, "Is justice good?" Socrates suggests that he will now follow that shift by coming to the defense of justice (347e4–348a6; compare pp. 86–87 above).

Still, even though Socrates suggests that he has thus far postponed following the shift initiated by Thrasymachus' shepherd speech, we should take a moment before we turn directly to Socrates' defense of the goodness of justice to think further about the ways in which this shift has already made itself felt. Before doing so, however, let us briefly address a question, for we may be struck that the line that Socrates draws here between Thrasymachus' claims about what justice is and his claims about whether justice is good (again 347e2–4) seems overly stark. Hasn't Thrasymachus been arguing about justice's (lack of) goodness from the very beginning? By defining justice as the advantage of the stronger, or locating justice in the service that the weak are commanded to do for the strong, it would certainly seem that Thrasymachus has implicitly attacked the common good, or the goodness of justice for the just, from the start.[44] What, then, does Socrates have in mind in drawing such a stark line? Perhaps even what we have just said indicates the most important point: it is not until his shepherd speech, as we also noted earlier, that

---

44. See pp. 65–66 above. On the implicit critique of the goodness of justice running *throughout* Thrasymachus' claims, beginning with his original definition of justice, see also Annas, *An Introduction*, pp. 36–47, and Nettleship, pp. 34–35. Benardete overstates when he says that "Thrasymachus started out with a definition of justice that seemingly was neutral on the issue of its goodness" (p. 26).

Thrasymachus *explicitly* denies the existence of the common good, that he says *explicitly* that justice is bad for the just (see pp. 80–81 above). This point is important, moreover, not only for understanding Thrasymachus' arguments, but also, and just as significantly, for understanding Socrates' different responses to Thrasymachus (and here we come to the ways in which the shift caused by Thrasymachus' speech has already made itself felt). Earlier in the discussion, prior to Thrasymachus' shepherd speech, Socrates tried to argue against Thrasymachus by portraying artisans, rulers, and knowers as simply devoted, in their activities, to the good of others, as simply selfless (see again, e.g., 342d3–e11). But now, in the wake of Thrasymachus' shepherd speech and its explicit assertion that justice is harmful to the just man himself, Socrates has clarified his portrait of artisans, rulers, and knowers in such a way that, as we have seen, he is no longer presenting or defending selfless devotion. Although he has not yet turned to defend the goodness of justice, Socrates has, we can say, already recognized the need to do so, and he has already accepted Thrasymachus' terms: Socrates has granted that the primary concern of every individual (at least judging by artisans, rulers, and knowers) is for his own good. To put this point slightly differently, once Thrasymachus has explicitly linked the question of justice to the question of the good—that is, the individual good or the most profitable life—Socrates may still oppose Thrasymachus' understanding of what that good consists of, but he does not deny, indeed he affirms, the necessity of considering matters from this perspective.

But what is this necessity? Why must justice, which presents itself as an independent, even the highest, standard, and which seems to call for our allegiance as a matter not of our own good but of duty or obligation, ultimately be judged and defended in terms of the individual good? This question may be the most important one arising from Socrates' entire discussion with Thrasymachus. Yet it is also difficult to answer, and it is hard to see how we can go beyond merely noting—how we can come to understand—Socrates' acceptance of Thrasymachus' terms. One step we can take, however, is to try to understand more fully just what "Thrasymachus' terms" are and how they have emerged from what we have seen thus far. For even Thrasymachus himself is more complicated than he is often thought to be—a complexity of which we have seen some indications—and it is important to grasp that the questions he raises are not simply those of an unjust man (see, e.g., pp. 85–86 above). To the brief review sketched in the preceding paragraph, then, let us add a final reflection on the main points of Thrasymachus' presentation thus far, beginning with his initial argument in which he spoke of the way cities are ruled (338d7–339a4). For we may recall that there was a kind of double meaning to that argument. Thrasymachus' argument, we suggested (pp. 68–69 and note 12 above), was meant not only as a praise of the rulers but also as an *accusation*. Thrasymachus accused the rulers of a fraud: the rulers dress up their own interests in the misleading name "justice." In accord with this, as we saw, Socrates too incurred Thrasymachus' wrath, both initially—when he seemed to be hiding his true thoughts or practicing a sycophantic hypocrisy—and later, when he seemed to be himself naively taken in by what the rulers say about justice. Thus, while Thrasymachus has attacked "justice," he has done so not entirely out of wickedness (or injustice) but partly out of a kind of justice of his own: he wants to expose the fraud, to show that when the rulers order the ruled to be just or to serve "the common good," the rulers are merely deceiving (and/or forcing) the ruled into serving their own private interests. Again, the rulers in the various cities are not themselves just. They are acting solely for the sake of their own good. Yet, in making this accusation, hasn't Thrasymachus (unwittingly) suggested or implied that *he himself* believes that there is a standard higher than the individual good? This would seem to be implicit in his indignation at the rulers for acting only on the basis of their own interests: just as one would not (with genuine indignation) accuse others of dishonesty unless one believed that people ought to be honest, or accuse others of cheating unless one believed that people ought to act fairly, so it would seem that one would not accuse the rulers of seeking their own good unless one believed—at least on some level—that they *ought* to act otherwise.[45] Now, throughout the conversation between Thrasymachus and Socrates, rulers have represented a kind of test

---

45. One might think that Thrasymachus' objection to the rulers is merely that they are hypocrites. But since the rulers' hypocrisy is dictated by a prudent calculation of their own interests (at least as Thrasymachus sees it), Thrasymachus' objection must run deeper, to the rulers' unwillingness to put any restraint on action in accord with this principle.

case for justice (see again, e.g., 338e1–339a4, 342e6–11, 343a7–d1, 347d2–e1). My suggestion can therefore be put another way: *Thrasymachus himself* thinks—at least on some level—that the rulers ought to be just, or, stated in terms more appropriate to his accusation, he thinks that they ought to put the common good before their own individual good in fact and not only in speech.

Needless to say, however, Thrasymachus has not quite been able to bring himself to say this. In fact, what he has explicitly said is quite the opposite. But why can't he bring himself to say this? What has prevented him from insisting on the obligation that his accusation of the rulers would seem to point to? With this question, we are now in a better position to understand the full significance of what comes to light in Thrasymachus' shepherd speech. For, as we noted above, this is where Thrasymachus makes fully explicit his belief that *there is no common good* and thus that the rulers would harm themselves by serving the ruled. That is, if Thrasymachus' opening presentation can be read as an insistence, in part, that the rulers do not act for the sake of the common good but that they *should*, the shepherd speech makes the problem deeper, because Thrasymachus has now openly argued that there is not even a potential common good that one could act for. Even if Thrasymachus has given signs, then, of a lingering belief that the rulers ought to be just, what prevents him from fully affirming this, from fully believing in this "ought," is his view that it would be foolish of the rulers to be just, and Thrasymachus proves unwilling to insist that anyone *ought* to be foolish, or that anyone could have an obligation to harm himself.

Now, one could say that Thrasymachus thus proves ultimately to be of very deficient justice. And this is in some sense surely true. But it is important to see where his commitment to justice breaks down. For it is not true that Thrasymachus is entirely unmoved by or unconcerned with justice, or that he simply refuses without a thought to allow anything to deter him from his pursuit of his own good. Rather, he sees—or thinks he sees—a flaw within justice itself. And as for the legitimacy of the question he raises, didn't we see in our earlier consideration of Socrates' exchanges with Cephalus and Polemarchus that justice itself promises to be good for the just? We saw, at any rate, the great weight Cephalus and Polemarchus—two men of much less ambiguous justice than Thrasymachus—placed on the goodness of justice, a weight so great, in fact, that it had a bearing in their minds too on the question of obligation. While Cephalus and Polemarchus were by no means led to Thrasymachus' conclusions, they too acknowledged, in a different way, that the question of justice's goodness is not a secondary question extrinsic and subordinate to the question of obligation. And in addition to looking back to Cephalus and Polemarchus, we should also look ahead to Glaucon, for Glaucon gives his own first acknowledgment of the same point by presently expressing his belief in the goodness of justice and his desire to see it defended against Thrasymachus' attack (see 347e4–348a6).

Socrates' Three-Argument Defense of Justice (347e4–354a11)

So Socrates turns to argue that justice is good for the individual, or that the just life is better than the unjust life. His defense of justice takes up the rest of Book One, and it is undertaken primarily, it seems, for the sake of Glaucon, who entered the conversation when the topic turned to ruling (see 347e4–6 and 348a4–5). By his own account, Glaucon has not been persuaded by Thrasymachus that the unjust life is better than the just life, even though he has heard all the good things Thrasymachus has attributed to the unjust life (347e7–348a3). Yet, although Glaucon expresses his continued confidence in justice, this does not mean that Thrasymachus' attack on justice has not made any impression on him, for he eagerly jumps at Socrates' proposal that they should try to find a way to refute Thrasymachus (348a4–6). Promising Glaucon, then, that he (or they?) will defend justice, Socrates lets Glaucon decide the procedure by which this defense will be conducted. Socrates gives Glaucon two choices: they can alternate long speeches with Thrasymachus and respond to his lists of all the good things belonging to the unjust life by extolling the goods of the just life, in which case they will have to count and measure all the good things in each of the speeches and there will be need of judges (348a7–b2), or the discussion can proceed as it did just a moment ago, by reaching agreements, and thus they can dispense with the need for judges other than themselves (348b2–4). Glaucon chooses the latter method, the one that we may call dialectical. The great advantage of this method would seem to be that by moving from agreed-upon premises to conclusions accepted by all the participants, it can produce firmer and more genuine agreements. But this method also runs a certain risk, for if the premises that are agreed upon are flawed, as they very well may be by this method, the conclusions that are reached may be spurious. We have said that Socrates' defense of justice is undertaken largely for the sake of Glaucon. We will have to wonder what effect it is meant to have on him. Is it meant to be convincing, or does it have some other purpose?

As we have already said, the general aim of Socrates' defense of justice is to show the goodness of justice for the individual, to vindicate the just life in these terms (see again 344e1–b3, 347e2–348a5). His defense is divided, however, into three arguments, each of which takes up some specific topic or aspect of "how justice stands in comparison with injustice" (351a1–2). The particular points Socrates tries to get Thrasymachus to concede in his three arguments are respectively: (1) that the just man is wise and good whereas the unjust man is ignorant and bad, (2) that justice is stronger than injustice, and (3) that the just are happier and live better than the unjust, and hence that justice is more profitable than injustice. Now, among other things this list will require us to consider—e.g., Why these particular topics? and, What is their relation to one another?—one thing we ought to note here at the outset is that not every topic Socrates takes up is one Thrasymachus explicitly raised in his attack on justice. In particular, the topic of Socrates' first argument, how justice and injustice compare in terms of wisdom and virtue, was not in any obvious way a part of Thrasymachus' attack. Thus, Socrates must do some preliminary work before his first argument in order to get Thrasymachus to formulate his position in these terms.

Socrates accomplishes this through a brief exchange that is a kind of prelude to his defense of justice, ostensibly designed to get Thrasymachus to clarify his position. In this exchange, Socrates gets Thrasymachus to acknowledge that he would put injustice in the class of virtue and wisdom and justice in the class of their opposites (348e1–4). He does so by beginning from Thrasymachus' claim that injustice is more profitable than justice; for Thrasymachus proves to be influenced by a certain thought that connects the question of profit with that of virtue—the thought, that is, that true virtue must be something good and thus profitable for the one who possesses it.

When Socrates asks him, after revisiting his claim that injustice is more profitable than justice, whether he would call justice virtue and injustice vice, Thrasymachus responds sarcastically, "That's likely, you delightful man, seeing as how I say that injustice is profitable and justice isn't" (348c5–8). Rather than calling justice virtue and injustice vice, Thrasymachus says that he would say "the opposite" (348c10). It is true that Thrasymachus does show some reluctance to call justice vice (see 348c11–12). But when pressed by Socrates' further questioning about his admiration of the unjust man (348d3–9), Thrasymachus accepts the position that sets injustice in the class (*merei*) of virtue and wisdom, and justice in the class of their opposites: "I certainly do set them down that way" (348e1–4).

With Thrasymachus' position now formulated in this way, Socrates pauses for a few final remarks before turning directly to his defense of justice. Strikingly, he praises Thrasymachus for the consistency of the position he has just accepted (348e5–349a2). Thrasymachus is more consistent, Socrates says, than those who maintain that injustice is profitable and yet still concede that it is shameful, thereby implying that shamefulness and harm—and hence by implication virtue and profit, or the noble and the good—need not cohere (348e6–9). Socrates says that it is harder to respond to Thrasymachus than it would be to respond to such a position, because in the latter case one could appeal to "the conventional things" (*ta nomizonta*): with those (probably more than a few) who doubt that justice is profitable without doubting that it is virtue, one could look at what is meant by virtue and ask whether it could really be something harmful.[46] Thrasymachus' more extreme position, by contrast, is "more solid" (348e5) and thus seems impressive for its greater rigor and coherence. By offering Thrasymachus this praise, however, Socrates also calls attention to the unconventionality of Thrasymachus' position. If Thrasymachus' position is less vulnerable to an argument that would question the separation of the noble and the good, it is, by virtue of the very same extremism that makes it consistent, a position that is publicly very questionable. And indeed it is worth noticing that when he is put on the spot by Socrates to affirm that he really believes what he says, Thrasymachus does show a dis-

---

46. Compare Plato, *Laws* 661d6–663a8, *Gorgias* 474c4–475c9; see also Friedländer, p. 64; Irwin, *Plato's Ethics*, pp. 177, 180; Nettleship, p. 35.

cernible uneasiness with being associated with his position as it now stands (see 349a4–10).[47] Thrasymachus' uneasiness here, which is perhaps prompted or exacerbated by Socrates' highlighting of the unconventionality of his position, may help to explain something that is otherwise puzzling about this brief exchange, namely, *why* Socrates brings up the topic of virtue. This is puzzling, to begin with, because by pushing Thrasymachus to make his position more radical and "more solid," Socrates seems, as he himself suggests, to be making his task in defending justice only that much more difficult. Yet, although Socrates may be making his task more difficult in one sense, we now see that he has also positioned himself as the defender of the conventional opinion that justice is virtue. In his first argument, Socrates will overturn the position Thrasymachus has just taken and replace it with the concession that the just man is wise and good whereas the unjust man is ignorant and bad. And perhaps this is the best place to note and try to understand the remarkable effect Socrates' first argument has on Thrasymachus. It is this argument that causes Thrasymachus to blush his famous blush, and in addition, it is after this

---

47. Thrasymachus' uneasiness here makes it all the more remarkable that he is nonetheless willing to take the position he does. By taking such a publicly questionable position, Thrasymachus shows a certain willingness to stick his neck out for the cause of injustice, exposing himself to contempt for defending a view so opposed to conventional opinion. In connection with this, it is perhaps worth stressing again that Thrasymachus has just agreed to a description of injustice by which it is not only profitable but also strong and noble; in fact, he has even agreed that he would attribute to injustice *all* of the characteristics "we" typically attribute to justice as a virtue (see 348e5–349a3; see also 344c4–6, 340d1–341a4, and 351b4–c3). Finally—a third point perhaps tied to these other two—we should note here that Thrasymachus will soon go on to speak of the unjust man as believing in a kind of desert: he believes that he is "worthy of" (*axioi*) getting the better of everyone else, just and unjust alike (see 349c4–10). In sum, it is another aspect of the complicated puzzle of Thrasymachus, of his distorted or perverted but not entirely vanished concern for virtue, that he displays a quasi-virtuous belief in the cause of injustice. Perhaps Thrasymachus' strange excessiveness in this direction, though, is an indication that the hopes most men place in justice have not entirely disappeared in his soul—which may not be such a surprise given the inadequacy of his critique of justice—but have somehow been transferred to the image of the perfectly unjust man who has the strength, virtue, and knowledge to guarantee his own good (see 348d5–8; reconsider also 340d1–341a4, 343e7–344c8, and see 351b1–c3).

argument that Thrasymachus opts out of the discussion, at least in the sense of offering serious resistance. He decides, as he himself puts it, that he will henceforth merely shake and nod his head and say "fine" to Socrates' questions as if he were humoring an old woman telling a tale (350e1–7). Now, Thrasymachus' reaction to Socrates' argument is surprising because, as we will see, Socrates' first argument is a very poor argument and Thrasymachus is clearly not convinced by it. Furthermore, Thrasymachus has previously responded to Socrates' faulty arguing with either anger at Socrates' perceived trickery or frustration at his perceived naiveté (see, e.g., 336b7–d4, 341a5–c3, and 343a3–d3). Why does Thrasymachus react to Socrates' first argument in this section so differently, by feeling embarrassment and shame instead? It may be that by defending, even if speciously, or perhaps *especially* if speciously, the conventional opinion that justice is virtue, Socrates finally succeeds in teaching Thrasymachus a certain lesson at least about prudence. I say that this lesson may follow especially if Socrates' argument is specious, because taking the topic of Socrates' argument together with the fact that Socrates' argument is too flawed to be seriously intended, Thrasymachus may thus come to see that Socrates is not being merely tricky, and surely not naive, but much more prudent than he is. Whatever may be Socrates' own deepest views, his virtuosity and prudence in giving at least rhetorical support to conventional opinion may bring home to Thrasymachus his own foolishness in openly declaring his own most unconventional thoughts.[48]

Now, Socrates' desire to teach Thrasymachus such a lesson may go much of the way toward explaining why Socrates leads the discussion to the question of virtue, but it does not go the entire way. We must also briefly consider the basic strategy of Socrates' defense of justice. We have already noted that Socrates' defense of justice is divided into three arguments that judge justice and injustice by standards that can now be stated more briefly as (1) virtue and wisdom, (2) strength, and (3) happiness and profit. Perhaps the most important observation to make about this list is that it is only in his third

---

48. For other explanations of Thrasymachus' blush compare Sallis, p. 343; Howland, p. 74; Bloom, p. 336; Benardete, p. 28; Annas, *An Introduction*, p. 52; and Nichols, p. 52 (and p. 203 n. 30).

argument that Socrates explicitly takes up the question of whether the just life is better than the unjust life; only this argument is introduced as being about "whether the just live better and are happier than the unjust" (352d2–3). Yet this is somewhat misleading, for there is an important connection tying at least Socrates' first and third arguments together. The crucial step in Socrates' third argument is based on the conclusion of his first argument: Socrates argues in his third argument that the just life is better than the unjust life, and that justice is thus more profitable than injustice, *because* justice is virtue. Indeed, in the broadest terms, this is the basic plan of Socrates' defense of justice: to approach the question of the happiness or profitability of the just life *via* the question of whether or not justice is virtue, to argue that justice is virtue and therefore that it is more profitable than injustice. This approach does, of course, make some immediate sense, on the simple grounds Thrasymachus himself has just recognized—namely, if something is true virtue, at least one thing that would seem to mean is that it is good (and thus profitable) for the one who possesses it. But this approach also poses a problem, for it means that Socrates' success in showing in his third argument that the just life is better than the unjust life depends on his success in showing in his first argument that justice is virtue. And, as has already been said, Socrates' first argument is a very poor argument.

Socrates' First Argument (349b1–350c11)

What then is Socrates' first argument? And what is wrong with it? Socrates' first argument is a long and intricate approach to the question of how justice and injustice compare in terms of virtue and wisdom. In fact, it takes *twenty-eight* steps in all for Socrates to replace Thrasymachus' position that injustice belongs in the class of virtue and wisdom, and justice in the class of their opposites, with the concession that the just man is good and wise whereas the unjust man is ignorant and bad (350c10–12). Since this argument is rather complicated, let me first give a brief summary of its basic movement through its four main stages.

   Socrates' argument begins, in its first stage (349b1–d2), by securing Thrasymachus' agreement to a point that even Thrasymachus himself had earlier stressed (cf. 343d3–344a6), namely, that the just man shows a restraint that the unjust man disregards. Whereas the just man is unwilling to get the better of (*pleonektein*) a fellow just man or to stray beyond (*pleonektein*) the just action, but thinks instead that he ought to get the better only of the unjust man, the unjust man, by contrast, thinks that he ought to get the better of everyone, just and unjust alike. This means, as Socrates reformulates it, that the just man does not get the better of (*pleonektein*) what is like him but only of what is unlike him, while the unjust man gets the better of like as well as unlike. Thrasymachus is quite pleased by this result, and so Socrates turns, in the second stage of his argument (349d3–12), to Thrasymachus' opinion that the unjust man is prudent and good while the just man is neither of these things. Does this mean, Socrates asks, that the unjust man is like the prudent and good, while the just man is not like them? When Thrasymachus assents to this odd and seemingly redundant question (see 349d8–9), Socrates then asks, "Then is each of them such as those whom he is like?" to which Thrasymachus also gives his assent, having in mind men whom he has already said are identical. That is, Thrasymachus agrees that "each of them is such as those whom he is like" because he has in mind the identity, which he has just asserted, of the unjust and the prudent and good. This agreement, however, provides the principle or premise on which Socrates can go on to refute Thrasymachus. For, turning in the third stage of his argument (349d13–350b2) to the model of artisans and their unwillingness to get the better of (*pleonektein*) their fellow artisans in the practice of their arts, Socrates is able to force Thrasymachus to agree that those who know are not willing to get the better of others who know but only of those who do not know. And since Thrasymachus also agrees that the one who knows is wise, and that the one who is wise is good, Socrates can thus conclude, in the forth and final stage of his argument (350b3–c12), that the wise and good show a restraint akin to that of the just man: they are not willing to get the better of (*pleonektein*) what is like them but only of what is unlike them, while the ignorant and bad, like the unjust, are willing to get the better of both like and unlike alike. This means, then, that there is a likeness between the wise and good and the just, and between the ignorant and bad and the unjust. And if "each of them is such as those whom he is like," the final result follows: the just man is good and wise whereas the unjust man is ignorant and bad.

Admittedly, Socrates' argument is somewhat more intricate than this summary may suggest, but this intricacy serves primarily to confuse Thrasymachus and to help trick him, most importantly to help trick him into agreeing and allowing that "each of them is such as those whom he is like." This principle, which gets introduced inconspicuously and in the context, as we noted above, of Thrasymachus' prior assertion of the identity of the unjust and the prudent and good, is essential to the success of Socrates' argument. Only by means of this principle does the penultimate conclusion (established through many steps) that there is a *likeness* between the just man and the wise and good, and a *likeness* between the unjust man and the ignorant and bad, get turned into the final conclusion that the just man *is* wise and good, and the unjust man *is* ignorant and bad. Yet it is not hard to see that there is a problem here. For the principle "each of them is such as those whom he is like" clearly should not be used as Socrates uses it, that is, as the general principle that any similarity between two types of people *not yet known to be identical* must mean that they are identical ("If x is like y, then x is y"). A moment's reflection—think of any two types that share a partial similarity (the dead and the asleep, for instance)—is enough to see the flaw in this principle. By bringing out, then, merely a certain similarity between the just and the wise and good, a similar restraint each shows in getting the better of (*pleonektein*) what is like, Socrates has not shown that the just man is wise and good. (There are many other things, of course, to being wise and good than any restraint it might involve, and Socrates' argument does nothing to show that these other things belong to the just as well as to the wise and good.)

In addition, there is a further difficulty with Socrates' argument, one that is less obvious but worthy of more reflection. For even the similarity between the just and the wise and good that Socrates brings out is not unquestionable or unambiguous; it is not clear that Socrates succeeds in showing that the just man's restraint is of exactly the same character as the restraint that the wise and good show. Crucial here is the Greek term *pleonektein*, which I translated in my summary of Socrates' argument (with one exception) as "to get the better of," but which has a range of meanings, from "to exploit" or "to take advantage of," on the one hand, to "to exceed" or "to go beyond," on the other. This range of meanings is essential to Socrates' argument because it enables him to move, with apparent seamlessness, from the unwillingness of the just man to take advantage of (*pleonektein*) his fellow just men, to a parallel with the artisan's unwillingness to exceed (*pleonektein*) his fellow artisans in the performance of his art, and from there to an equation with the unwillingness of the wise and good to exceed (*pleonektein*) what is like.[49] By using the same term here, however, Socrates may obscure some important differences: Is the just man's restraint, that is, his unwillingness to take advantage of his fellow just men because it would be unjust or wrong to do so (see 349b2–c3), really equivalent to an artisan's restraint, which consists of his unwillingness to surpass his fellow artisans because it would be artless or foolish to do so (see 349d13–350a10)? As Socrates presents the arts in this argument, the only restraint they appear to call for seems to be based, not on anything like duty or devotion, but simply on each artisan's knowledge of some standard—for example, harmony or health—that it would be foolish to overshoot (see especially 349e10–350a9). Such restraint seems to be of a different character than the moral restraint required by justice. And if there is indeed a difference here between justice and the arts, this difference is significant because the suggestion conveyed by the movement of Socrates' argument (from the arts to knowledge to wisdom to virtue) is that true wisdom and virtue would be closer, in whatever restraint might be involved, to the arts than to justice.[50]

In light of these difficulties with Socrates' argument, it should come as no surprise that Socrates soon states the result of this argument this way: "*If in fact* justice is wisdom and virtue . . ." (351a3–4, emphasis added).

---

49. On Socrates' manipulation of the range of *pleonektein*, compare Pappas, p. 46; Annas, *An Introduction*, p. 51; and Cross and Woozely, p. 52.

50. Contrast Nettleship, pp. 36–40, who unites justice and the arts under the banner of living in accordance with "limits." Nettleship's argument, however, that justice and the arts both represent limits in the sense of "perfections," does not give sufficient weight to the possible difference in the meaning of these limits; above all, his argument rests on the questionable claim that for "the Greeks" virtue—be it virtue in general or justice in particular—"is not a moral conception" and that "law" never carried the sense of "the moral law." Contrast, for example, Xenophon, *Oeconomicus*, sec. VII–VIII.

Socrates' Second Argument (350e11–352d2)

As I mentioned earlier, it is after Socrates' first argument that Thrasymachus blushes and that he declares he will no longer answer seriously; from now on, he says, he will just shake and nod his head and say "fine" as if he were humoring an old woman telling a tale (350e2–4). It is true, to be fair, that Thrasymachus does offer to give a speech in response to Socrates' first argument, with which he may see the problems once he has had a moment to reflect (350d9–e1). But Socrates does not take Thrasymachus up on this offer. Nor, we should note, does he object very strenuously to Thrasymachus' decision to treat him like an old woman by merely shaking and nodding his head and saying "fine" (see 350e8–9). If Socrates' first argument, especially with the acceptance of "each of them is such as those whom he is like," gave us a good example of the potential shortcomings of the dialectical method, we are led now to expect nothing more than a farcical version of that method, and we must wonder what purpose Socrates has in mind in allowing the discussion to take this turn.

Furthermore, we must also wonder about Socrates' selection of the topic for his second argument. We have already noted that there is a connection between Socrates' first and third arguments. But where does his second argument fit into his defense of justice? Socrates introduces his second argument—having supposedly just shown in his first that justice is wisdom and virtue, and injustice ignorance and vice—by saying that they should turn now to Thrasymachus' still unrefuted claim that justice is "stronger" (*ischvroteron*) than injustice (see 350d6–7, 351a2–5). Unlike his first argument, then, it seems that Socrates' second argument will take up a specific claim made in Thrasymachus' shepherd speech. Yet Socrates refers here to a part of Thrasymachus' speech in which Thrasymachus made a number of claims, only one of which was that injustice is stronger than justice. Thrasymachus claimed in the very same sentence that injustice, at least when it is committed on a sufficient scale, is also "freer" and "more masterful" than justice (see 344c4–6). Why is Socrates taking up only one of Thrasymachus' claims? And why this one?[51] In addi-

---

51. It is possible that Socrates is referring to 348e9–349a3 rather than 344c4–6, for at 348e9–349a3 Thrasymachus again accepted the view that injustice

tion to these questions, we should also note that Socrates explicitly separates his second argument from his first. As Socrates himself points out, if one accepts the view that justice is wisdom and virtue, then it would seem a small step from there to the conclusion that justice is stronger than injustice (351a3–5). But Socrates says that he does not want the question of the strength of justice to be examined "so simply," but rather "in the following way," that is to say, in a way independent of his first argument (351a6–7). Why does Socrates make a point of separating his second argument from his first?

We can make some headway at least on this last question as soon as we begin to examine Socrates' second argument. For, far from beginning from the conclusion that justice is wisdom and virtue, this argument has the task of making the case for the necessity of justice as something distinct from wisdom (if not necessarily distinct from virtue as well). That this is at least implicitly the task of Socrates' second argument can be seen if we consider this argument in light of Thrasymachus' response to the second question that Socrates asks in this section. Socrates begins by asking Thrasymachus this question: "Would you say that a city is unjust if it tries to enslave other cities unjustly, succeeds in reducing them to slavery, and has many enslaved to itself?" (351b1–3). Thrasymachus replies that of course he would say so and adds that this is what he thinks the best cities do (351b4–5). Then, as his second question, Socrates asks whether a city can become stronger than other cities if it lacks justice, to which Thrasymachus replies that a city needs justice to become strong only if, as Socrates has just been claiming, justice is wisdom, but if injustice is wisdom, as he maintains, then injustice is enough (351b6–c3). After this response, Socrates then goes on, in implicit opposition *not* to Thrasymachus' separation of justice and wisdom but to his claim that wisdom suffices, to make the case for the necessity of justice as well. Socrates points out that neither a city, nor an army, nor a group of pirates, nor a band of thieves, nor indeed any other group that wants to accomplish something unjust in common can succeed if its members behave unjustly toward one another

is strong. However, this is less likely since that view seemed in the later passage to be accepted merely as an implication of Thrasymachus' broader view that injustice belongs in the class of virtue—the view that was supposedly addressed in Socrates' first argument.

(351c8–d1). For injustice, he argues, produces factions, hatreds, and fights, whereas justice produces unanimity and friendship; consequently, no group can dispense entirely with justice and accomplish anything, even an unjust end (351d4–e1, 351e9–352a3, 352c1–8). In brief, then, Socrates' argument is simply this: any common enterprise, any community, requires justice at least among its members lest that enterprise, that community, be destroyed by internal strife.

Now, we may doubt that this argument is enough to fully support the conclusion that Socrates draws, namely, that justice is stronger than injustice, or that "the just appear more capable of action, while the unjust appear unable to do anything with one another" (352b7–c1). For this conclusion follows from Socrates' argument only if we are willing to call "just" those groups that possess merely the requisite justice to get along among themselves while they commit injustices against others. And while it may be reasonable of Socrates to insist that such groups are not wholly unjust but rather only "half corrupt with injustice" (352c7), that is short of saying that they are simply just. Still, it would seem hard to deny that there is at least *some* truth to what Socrates says in this argument. No common enterprise, it seems correct to say, can succeed, no community can exist, without some justice. The more important question, though, is how well this argument reflects on justice and communities. For one thing, Socrates presents justice in this argument merely as a means, and as a means even to unjust ends (see especially 351c8–10, 352c5–7). Justice so understood—belonging to a band of thieves as much as to any other community—may be necessary, but it also seems marred and diminished by its service to purposes that are not themselves guided or limited by justice.[52] Moreover, the question could arise in this context of how communities that are not themselves guided by justice can justly demand, as a genuine obligation, the justice they require of their members. And this question gains a particular importance when we consider that Socrates' argument, while showing the need for justice in a community *as a whole*, does not prove that *every single member* of a community must himself be just. Socrates' argument does not reach the individual who will quietly neglect his own duties to the community while profiting from the

---

52. See Bloom, p. 336; Benardete, p. 29; Strauss, *The City and Man*, p. 82.

fact that the community is still held together by the justice of his fellow members. It is true that Socrates does extend his argument to the individual by arguing that when injustice comes into being within one man it will produce within him the same strife and division that it produces within a community of men (351e6–352a8). But this extension of Socrates' argument depends on the highly questionable premise that injustice has a natural work that has the same form and effect within an individual's soul—a whole that is surely much more of a unity than any community of men—that it has in the relations among separate individuals with potentially competing interests. Socrates offers nothing more than an assertion in this argument that what the individual requires for his own internal harmony and order, the justice, if we should put it that way, by which his soul gets along with itself, perfectly coincides with and requires the justice that the community demands of him.[53]

Socrates' second argument does not help to show, then, that justice, understood here in its ordinary sense of performing one's duties to the community, is always good for the individual. In fact, we must go one step further and acknowledge that this argument even has implications in the opposite direction. For why else, other than that each individual's own contribution to a common enterprise is not in every case good for that individual, would wisdom not be enough to hold a group together and would justice therefore be necessary? We noted above that Socrates' argument, when set against the backdrop of Thrasymachus' claim to the effect that wisdom alone could hold a community together (again, 351c1–3), is an argument for the necessity of justice as something distinct from wisdom, an argument that justice is necessary to supply that which wisdom alone cannot produce. And yet wouldn't wisdom be sufficient to lead people to do anything that is good for them? In principle, or assuming that the individuals in a given common enterprise possess wisdom, justice would be necessary only if there is a need to get at least some of the individuals to do something that is harmful to them. As we put the same point in our earlier discussion of an exchange between Socrates and Polemarchus, justice as devotion to the common good is neces-

---

53. See Irwin, *Plato's Ethics*, pp. 178–179; Annas, *An Introduction*, p. 53; Reeve, pp. 20–21.

sary, in principle, only when there is no true common good in the strict sense.[54] And this is perhaps the deepest problem or paradox of Socrates' second argument, for it means that while Socrates may be able to make a strong case here for the necessity of justice in order to keep communities together or for the sake of "the common good," he can do so only at the expense of indicating what this necessity implies in terms of the individual good.[55]

Socrates' Third Argument (352d2–354a11)

After his second argument, Socrates introduces his third and final argument by saying that although he has already learned through his first two arguments that the just are wiser and better and more capable of action than the unjust, he must still examine the question of "whether the just live better and are happier than the unjust," a question, he says, "that is not about just any ordinary matter, but about the way one ought to live" (352d2–6 and preceding context). Socrates promises, in other words, that his third argument will directly take up the question of the individual good.[56]

That Socrates presents this as an open question may seem to make sense, for we have just seen that the strongest part of his second

---

54. See pp. 38–39 above. Consider also the implication of Cross and Woozely's objection to Socrates' argument: ". . . if Plato wants to suggest . . . that a gang of criminals cannot be kept together unless they recognize duties to each other, [this] seems patently untrue. A gang can be kept together by mutual fear, or by fear of the boss if he is a strong personality; or it can be kept together just by the continuous success of its exploits. In either case, a member has much to gain by staying in, and much to lose by trying to get out; and, as long as that is so, the gang will cohere" (p. 56). To the extent that Socrates has in fact made the case for the need for justice— and surely his argument is far from being "patently untrue"—he has also suggested that commitment to common enterprises is not always good for each individual. Surprisingly, Socrates' case for the need for justice is more "realistic," not to say pessimistic, about the possibility of securing a complete common good than Cross and Woozely's (and *Thrasymachus'*) "optimistic" denial of the need for justice. See also Benardete, p. 27.

55. This may be the appropriate place to note that this is the only one of Socrates' arguments with Thrasymachus that appeals to the gods and divine support for justice (see 352a10–b2).

56. See Sallis, p. 345.

argument casts less than favorable light on justice from the perspective of the individual good. Yet Socrates' opening statement here may still puzzle us if we think not only of Socrates' second argument but also of his first. If justice is wisdom and virtue, and injustice ignorance and vice, wouldn't it seem already to follow that the just life is better than the unjust life? It is true that Socrates himself says that this conclusion would appear to follow "from what we have said" (352d4–5). But he then immediately adds that this question remains in need of a better examination (352d5). Yet, rather than finding this odd, perhaps we ought to regard it as appropriate considering the weakness of Socrates' first argument: Socrates may be acknowledging that weakness here by presenting the question of the superiority of the just life as still unsettled and by calling for a better examination. If so, however, this serves only to underline the main difficulty we will soon confront, for Socrates' "better" examination in his third argument is not entirely separate from his first argument. As we noted earlier, Socrates' third argument does not simply stand on its own but relies in a crucial respect on his first argument.

To see in the first place just what Socrates' third argument is, but also to see where his first argument reappears, let us look at the basic movement of Socrates' third argument. In the broadest terms, this argument is an attempt to present a sketch of what the virtue of any given being is and then to apply this sketch to the human soul. Before approaching the general matter of virtue, however, Socrates begins from "work" (*ergon*), for he argues that the virtue of any given being is that which enables that being to do its work well. A horse, for instance, has a specific work (352d8–e1), and since a good horse is one that does the work of a horse well, it makes sense to say that whatever enables it to do so is the virtue of a horse. According to Socrates' presentation, then, one must first know the work of a being in order to determine its specific virtue. And the work of a being, Socrates says, is that which can be done only with that being or best with it (352e2–3). He gives the examples of eyes, ears, and a pruning knife: just as one can see only with eyes, so one can hear only with ears, and although one can cut a strip of vine with many different tools, one can do so most finely with a pruning knife designed for that purpose (352e5–353a11). Having thus explained "work," Socrates then goes on to virtue and explains it as we have already indicated—that is, given a certain being's specific work, the virtue of that being is that with which the being is able to do its work well and without which it cannot (353b2–d2). Socrates then applies this understanding of work and virtue to the soul. For the soul, as a being, must have a work (see 353d1). According to Socrates, "managing, ruling, deliberating, and all such things," are the work(s) of the soul, as is "living" too (353d3–9). Moreover, since the soul has a work, or works (see 353e1), the soul must therefore have a specific virtue with which it can do its work well and without which it cannot (353d11–e2).

Now, if we pause for a moment at this point in Socrates' argument, his line of reasoning may seem intelligible and straightforward enough. But before going any further, we should note that even what we have seen so far raises many more questions than it answers. For instance: Is the work and virtue of a being that is a whole, like a horse, so simply comparable to the work and virtue of a being that is part, like an eye, of another being? Which model—one of these, if they are two, or some third—would the soul fit? Is the soul a subordinate part of a human being, the whole of which includes body as well as soul?[57] Is the soul used, or is it a user? Can the several works Socrates attributes to the soul be reduced to a single work? If not, are there conflicts between the works and therefore multiple and competing virtues of the soul? If there are such conflicts, what determines the preeminent work and so the preeminent virtue? A number of these questions arise simply because the soul, unlike a horse or an eye, is such a difficult being to understand; the soul's work is not obvious and thus its virtue is hard to specify. To say that the soul's work is "living," for instance, may be acceptable as far as it goes, but it is extremely vague. What help could it provide in specifying the soul's virtue?

Socrates has a solution, however, to the difficulty of specifying the soul's virtue, a solution to which we have already alluded: "For didn't we agree," he asks Thrasymachus, "that justice is virtue of the soul, and injustice vice?" (353e7–8). That is, rather than deriving the

---

57. It is worth noting that Socrates' argument, especially in suggesting that living is the work of the soul alone, abstracts from the body. One result of this abstraction is that it will allow Socrates to suggest that the virtue of the soul guarantees happiness without having to take account of the bodily turns of fortune that might make even someone with an excellent soul miserable.

virtue of the soul from its work, Socrates simply refers at this crucial juncture to the conclusion of his first argument that justice is virtue, and injustice vice.[58] And by citing this earlier conclusion (slightly amended),[59] Socrates is able to draw a series of further conclusions. For if justice is the virtue of the soul, and living, as was just agreed, is the (or a) work of the soul, it follows from the sketch of work and virtue that Socrates has drawn that the just man must live well and the unjust man must live badly (353e10–12). Furthermore, Thrasymachus is also willing to agree that the one who lives well is happy and blessed, whereas the one who does not is miserable (354a1–3). The just man, Socrates can thus conclude, is happy, the unjust man miserable (354a4–5). And finally, since it is surely more profitable to be happy than to be miserable, it follows that "injustice is never more profitable than justice" (354a6–9).

These conclusions, moving from virtue to happiness to profit, complete Socrates' defense of justice and assert the final superiority of the just life to the unjust life. Needless to say, however, we cannot be satisfied, for while these conclusions may follow reasonably enough from one another, each of them can be only as sound as the primary one that justice is virtue of the soul. And since this primary conclusion—to repeat once again—is merely borrowed from Socrates' flawed first argument,[60] this is the crucial failing of Socrates' third argument: even if Socrates offers here a plausible sketch, broadly speaking, of what it would mean for something to be the virtue of the soul, and even if it is plausible, or even more than plausible, that one would be happier with such virtue than without it, this argument brings us no closer to an answer to the decisive question of whether this virtue is justice.

So Socrates' defense of justice does not convincingly show that the just life is good for the just man; it is a failure. Remarkably, even Socrates himself admits as much. After he has completed his third argument, Socrates expresses his dissatisfaction. Comparing himself

---

58. The reliance of Socrates' third argument on the conclusion of his first argument is noted also by Annas, *An Introduction*, p. 51, and Reeve, p. 21.

59. It should be noted that Socrates now simply tacks on "of the soul" to the conclusion that justice is virtue (cf. 350c10–11, d4–5). See Pappas, p. 49.

60. For the clearest flaw in Socrates' first argument, see p. 105 above.

to a greedy feaster who reaches for each new dish before having given the prior course its due tasting (354b1–3), he blames himself:

> Before finding out what we were examining first—what the just is—I let go of that to pursue the examination of whether [the just] is vice and ignorance or wisdom and virtue; and, in turn, when the subsequent argument burst in, that injustice is more profitable than justice, I could not restrain myself from going from the former one to this one. As a result, I have come to know nothing from this discussion. For so long as I don't know what the just is, I shall hardly know whether it happens to be a virtue or not, nor whether the one who possesses it is unhappy or happy. (354b4–c3)

These are the final words of Book One, and Socrates objects here to his entire discussion with Thrasymachus, or at least to the most important turn it took: Socrates says, in short, that he should not have turned to the question, "Is justice good?" since he had not yet answered the prior question, "What is justice?" In other words, he should not have defended justice before having adequately defined it. Socrates' statement, however, is also more specific than this, and we may wonder whether some of its specifics are not indications that Socrates is aware not only of the broad procedural problem of defending justice before defining it but also of the internal flaws in his defense of justice. For Socrates' statement, we should note, speaks not only of the questions, "What is justice?" and "Is justice good?" but also of the question of whether justice is vice and ignorance or wisdom and virtue, *which he separates from* the question of whether justice is profitable and makes its possessor happy, a question he portrays as having arisen *later*.[61]

Let us consider this last aspect of Socrates' statement first, namely, that Socrates presents the question of whether justice is profitable and conducive to happiness as having arisen *after* the question of, to abbreviate, wisdom and virtue. If Socrates' final statement is read strictly as a summary of the order of his entire discussion with

---

61. Here and in what follows, I take the questions of whether justice is profitable and makes its possessor happy as equivalent to the question, "Is justice good?"

Thrasymachus, this statement seems strangely misordered. For the question of profit and happiness first arose, or at least it became fully explicit, with Thrasymachus' attack on justice in his shepherd speech (see pp. 80–81, 86–87, and 94–95 above); as we saw, it was only through the subsequent efforts of Socrates that the question of wisdom and virtue was raised (see pp. 99–100 above). Yet, on the other hand, if Socrates is referring here to the order of his defense of justice more specifically, what he says makes more sense: in Socrates' defense of justice, the question of wisdom and virtue *did* in fact precede the question of profit and happiness. Socrates may be reminding us here in his final statement that it was the basic strategy of his defense of justice to approach the question of profit and happiness via the question of wisdom and virtue, to establish in this first argument that justice is virtue and then to spell out in his third argument how this leads to the conclusion that justice is profitable and makes its possessor happy. We considered this basic strategy earlier (see pp. 102–103 above), and we also observed that it seemed in keeping with the simple notion, implicit in what we think virtue is, that virtue must be good for the one who possesses it, a notion that gets a somewhat more theoretical expression in Socrates' third argument. However, if Socrates' final statement is alluding to the strategy of his defense of justice, it might then seem odd that this statement should *separate* the question of wisdom and virtue from the question of profit and happiness. Aren't these interconnected parts of the attempt to show the goodness of the just life? Yet this separation too makes sense (as did a similar separation at the beginning of Socrates' third argument: see 352b6–7, c8–d6) if we take it as a recognition on Socrates' part that his first argument was a failure. Not having shown in his first argument that justice is virtue, Socrates has not really addressed the question of profit and happiness by the beginning of his third argument. And of course he never really addresses this question—at least not adequately—since his third argument moves from virtue to profit and happiness without any new attempt to show that justice is virtue. This is only a restatement of the basic failure of Socrates' defense of justice, but Socrates' final statement may help us to confirm that Socrates is well aware of the reasons for that failure. As a final piece of evidence that Socrates' statement may be taken as confirmation of his awareness of the flaws in his defense of justice, we should note one further peculiarity: Socrates makes no mention in this statement of his second argument that justice is stronger than injustice. By excluding this argument, the argument in which he made the case for the necessity of justice for communities, Socrates may be acknowledging that in a certain sense this argument does not even belong to his defense of justice, at least not in the same way his other two arguments do. For this was the argument, we recall, that not only did not help in the attempt to show that justice is good for the individual but in a certain respect even hindered that attempt (see pp. 110-111 above).

Yet, if Socrates is as aware as he seems to be of the problems in his defense of justice, this makes it all the more important to confront a question that has been gaining steam throughout Socrates' defense of justice. For especially, we can now add, if he is aware of its problems, *why* does Socrates give such a poor defense of justice? I want to conclude this chapter by reflecting on this question and also by trying to think a bit further about the broader significance of Socrates' final remarks.

In his own objection to his procedure, the most obvious explanation that Socrates himself seems to give of his defense of justice is that he was too eager to refute Thrasymachus' attack on justice (354b4–9). This appears to be Socrates' explanation at any rate of why he turned from the question of what justice is to the attempt to defend the goodness of justice in the first place. But this explanation does not, of course, fully answer the question of why Socrates gives such a *poor* defense of justice. Even in his haste, Socrates easily could have come up with something better than what he offers. In fact, Socrates' defense of justice is so poor that it raises the alternative possibility that Socrates' intention was not so much to refute Thrasymachus, which, we recall, he was supposedly doing for the sake of Glaucon (see again 347e4–348b7 and pp. 98–99 above), as it was to provoke Glaucon. Socrates' poor defense of justice in Book One, by provoking Glaucon's demand that he give a better defense (see especially 357a2–b2), provides the push that sets the rest of the *Republic* in motion, which may have been something Socrates wanted to do (cf., however, 357a1).

This may be much of the reason, then, for the character of Socrates' defense of justice, and it would explain his willingness to give poor arguments on behalf of justice. We may still wonder, however, whether there is not also some further consideration that explains not only why Socrates gives poor arguments but also why he gives the specific poor arguments that he does. Let us return one last time to the problems in Socrates' defense and compare very briefly but more directly than we have so far the main problem of Socrates' second argument with the main problem of his first and third. Socrates' second argument, we should recall, begins from something that sounds a lot like justice as it is ordinarily understood: commitment or devotion to the common good that binds a community together. But it fails to show that justice so understood is always good for the individual; indeed it even has implications in the opposite direction, as we have mentioned. Socrates' first and third arguments, by contrast, sketch out something that sounds a lot like it would be good for the individual: wisdom and virtue, with virtue understood as that which enables one's soul to do its work well and thereby makes one happy. But the great failure of these arguments is to show that this virtue (or wisdom and virtue) is justice. Putting these failings together—that is, the failing of Socrates' second argument on the one hand, and that of his first and third on the other— may be a way of formulating the problem of justice: while we can easily find something that looks like justice, devotion to the common good that binds a community together, it is not so clear that this will always be good for the individual; so too, while we might be able to find (if perhaps less easily) what is good for the individual, it is not so clear that this will be justice. The juxtaposition of Socrates' second with his first and third arguments foreshadows and is meant, I suggest, to provide a preliminary presentation of a problem at the heart of the *Republic*. The later search for justice in Books Two through Four results in two different understandings of justice: doing one's job in the city on the one hand (see 433a1–434c10, cf. 420b3– 421c6), and setting one's soul in order on the other (see 441d5– 444a2; consider 434d2–435a3).

Socrates' defense of justice in Book One is "poor" in the specific ways it is poor, then, according to my suggestion, because it is intended to pose and to help us to reflect on the problem of justice. The problem, to repeat, is that what we ordinarily take to be justice is of questionable goodness for the individual, and what we might be able to show to be good for the individual is not so clearly justice. Now, when the problem is put this way, we might discern a certain relationship between the two main questions that have guided the discussion throughout Book One, the questions, "What is justice?"

and "Is justice good?" We should recall that Socrates' own complaint about his procedure in Book One, in the broadest meaning of his final statement, was that he should have discovered what justice is before considering whether or not it is good. This implies, of course, that the questions, "What is justice?" and "Is justice good?" are separable and ought to be kept distinct from one another. Yet it would seem from the way I have just posed what I am calling the problem of justice that these two questions may not be so separable. The problem, again, with what we ordinarily take to be justice is that its goodness is questionable. This seems to imply that if what we ordinarily take to be justice were not of questionable goodness, there would not be such a problem; we would be content to call that justice and leave matters at that. Perhaps we might even say that the question of what justice is arises as a question, above all, when doubts arise (and are not easily removed) about the goodness of what we ordinarily take to be justice. This seems to be borne out when we remember that the whole search for a definition of justice in Book One began when Socrates called into doubt the goodness of what Cephalus and Polemarchus understood justice to consist in.[62] If what we ordinarily take to be justice is not always good, there seems to be a need to search for what is always good and to call that justice. Much of the later movement of the *Republic*—especially that strand that leads to the definition of justice as the proper order of the soul and then on to the subsequent discussion of philosophy—can be understood along these lines, as a search driven by such an impetus.

---

62. There is a complication here that was also noted at the beginning of this chapter, namely that the doubts that Socrates cast on Cephalus' and Polemarchus' understandings of justice seemed in the first place to be doubts about whether justice so understood is good for those whom the just man helps, that is, the recipients of justice. Yet, as I suggested in chapter 1, the conviction that justice is good, and the power this conviction has in raising and pushing the question of what justice is, extends to and is perhaps even the greatest in the case of the just man himself (see pp. 54–55 above). The most significant indication of this may have been Polemarchus' expression of his conviction that justice is human virtue (see 335c4–5 and context). For one of the reasons, and perhaps the most powerful one, that we are dissatisfied with calling something that is not always good "justice" is our conviction that justice is (a) virtue. This conviction, in other words, is a crucial element of our insistence that justice be good. In this connection, see again Dobbs, "The Piety of Thought," pp. 678–679, and n. 19.

The only difficulty with this, however, just to restate the other horn of the dilemma, is that one might then wonder whether what is discovered in such a search, that which is discovered to be good, is justice, when the only true connection it seems to have to justice as justice is ordinarily understood is that it fulfills the demand or the wish that justice be good. In other words, if we are led away from justice as it is ordinarily understood in search of something else, what we find, while good, may no longer intelligibly warrant the name "justice." In light of this aspect of the problem, there might be a certain justification for, and this might even be the deeper meaning of, Socrates' suggestion in his final statement here in Book One that the question of what justice is ought to be separated from the question of whether justice is good—a suggestion that would seem to allow for the possibility of defining justice and then subsequently finding out that justice is not always good. And we should also note, more simply, that while Socrates' final statement is a criticism of his discussion with Thrasymachus, it also agrees in an important respect with the very development it criticizes. For Socrates allows here that the question, "Is justice good?" is at least at some point an essential and meaningful question; that is, he grants that one should not simply insist that justice must be good and define it in any way whatsoever so as to ensure that it is good. In this way as well, Socrates' statement would seem to indicate a qualified return to the ordinary understanding of justice, or at least a recognition of the difficulty in following the impetus that leads away from it.

Chapter 3

Glaucon and Adeimantus and Justice as the Proper Order of the Soul

Our study of Book One of the *Republic* has ended less with a solution than with the articulation of a problem. Socrates' final remarks at the end of Book One, I have just suggested, indicate a certain movement back toward accepting the ordinary understanding of justice as the best answer to the question of what justice is. Yet, with doubt having been cast on the goodness of justice so understood, this "solution" is not entirely satisfactory either. For even if we recognize the questionableness of redefining justice so as to ensure its goodness, it would seem to remain essential to what we think justice is that it be something good. When we consider that there is thus a difficulty besetting either a radical redefinition of justice on the one hand or a return to the ordinary understanding on the other, the general problem with which Book One culminates can be restated in the form of this question: Is there in fact a genuine whole that incorporates everything we think about justice, including both that it has the form and direction we ordinarily suppose it to have, i.e., that it is directed to the common good, and also that it is good for each of us as individuals?

Now, I mentioned at the end of the last chapter that this problem gets spelled out—but perhaps not fully resolved—in the rest of the *Republic*. The rest of the *Republic*, however, is not simply a repetition of Book One on a grander scale. There would seem to be at least one important difference we must reflect on. I have just suggested, to repeat, that Book One ends with a certain acceptance on Socrates' part of the ordinary understanding of justice, albeit an acceptance mitigated by an awareness of the problem of the goodness of justice so understood. Yet, if this suggestion is correct, what are we to make of the fact that the rest of the *Republic* seems to move in the opposite direction? For the most manifest definition of justice offered by the rest of the *Republic* is that justice is tending to the proper order of one's own soul. This is the definition Socrates "discovers" near the end of Book Four when, after first discovering justice in the city as each member doing his or her own task, he turns to apply this model to the individual soul and argues that justice is the proper relation of the soul's various parts, with reason ruling over spiritedness and desire (434d2–444a2). Although this latter definition is modeled on or patterned after justice in the city, it ultimately seems to win out—as true justice—over that contender, a contender that it is safe to say is a closer reflection of the ordinary understanding of justice. Justice in the city becomes only a "phantom" of justice, according to Socrates, when compared to justice in the soul (see 443b7–d1).

Yet the difficulties with understanding the proper order of the soul as a satisfactory definition of justice are several. Does a well-ordered soul necessarily issue in actions that contribute to the community, as we ordinarily understand justice to do? And even if it does issue in such actions, doesn't it make a difference in what spirit these actions are performed, that is, whether they are performed with the community in view and out of devotion to it or whether there is just a fortunate coincidence of interests between the soul and the community? These are difficulties that we have already touched on, in other versions, when Socrates made a few steps in Book One toward such an understanding of justice (see pp. 105–106, 113, and 118–120 above). For this reason, among others, it makes more sense to complete our study, not by dwelling on the shortcomings of this definition of justice, but by trying to see what leads Socrates to define justice in this way and how this definition can be justified, even if only partially. Is it simply arbitrary or absurd to define justice in this way?[1]

---

1. The riddle-like character of Socrates' definition has been noted by many. For other discussions of it see, for example, Annas, *An Introduction*, pp. 153–169; David Sachs, "A Fallacy in Plato's *Republic*," *Philosophical Review* 72 (1963): 141–158; In Ha Jang, "The Problematic Character of Socrates' Defense of Justice in Plato's *Republic*," *Interpretation* 24 (1996): 85–107; Irwin, *Plato's Moral Theory* (Oxford: Oxford University Press, 1977), pp. 208–212; Jerome Schiller, "Just Men and Just Acts in Plato's *Republic*," *Journal of the History of Philosophy* 6 (1968):

Now, although some basis for the *Republic*'s redefinition of justice has surely been laid in Book One—inasmuch as Book One has brought out the difficulties in the ordinary understanding of justice—it is important to stress that Socrates does not seek out a new definition of justice immediately after Book One but does so only after the speeches of Glaucon and Adeimantus. Glaucon's and Adeimantus' speeches at the beginning of Book Two serve as a kind of bridge between Book One and the rest of the *Republic*, expressing understandable dissatisfaction with Socrates' defense of justice and hope for a better defense. Glaucon and Adeimantus provide at once the final pieces of the presentation of the problem of justice at the beginning of the *Republic*, "resurrecting" and restating Thrasymachus' case against justice (see 358b7–c1, 367a5–8), and the first step into the rest of the *Republic*, laying out an agenda meant to dictate how Socrates is to defend justice (see 358b4–7, c8–d6, 367a8–e5). Before saying anything more, then, about the question of justice understood as the proper order of the soul, or as a way of further preparing the ground for that question, let me lay out briefly what I take to be the most significant aspects of Glaucon's and Adeimantus' speeches. I shall focus primarily on Glaucon's speech, both because it presents matters more starkly and thus more clearly than Adeimantus' and because Adeimantus himself presents his speech primarily as a supplement to Glaucon's (see 362e1–4).

Glaucon's and Adeimantus' Speeches (357a1–367e5)

Glaucon and Adeimantus make a remarkable request of Socrates, asking to be shown not merely that justice is good or profitable but that it is the greatest good of the soul. If the most successful result of Socrates' defense of justice in Book One was to show that justice holds communities together and makes them more capable of concerted action for the sake of other ends, such a mercenary defense of

---

1–14; Reeve, pp. 235–273; Gregory Vlastos, *Platonic Studies*, 2nd ed. (Princeton: Princeton University Press, 1981), pp. 110–139; Strauss, *The City and Man*, pp. 108–110, 115, 127, and "The Origins of Political Science and the Problem of Socrates," pp. 160–162; Bloom, pp. 375–379; Nichols, pp. 57–59, 91–97; Averroes, pp. 48–56.

justice, turning justice into a regrettable price to be paid for other goods, is not satisfactory to Glaucon and Adeimantus. It is not satisfactory, first of all, because any defense of justice in terms of the other goods it can procure would seem to contain an escape clause for any reflective and capable individual: the other goods one can procure through justice are procured more through the *appearance* of justice than through justice itself. Wouldn't it be better, then, to forget about justice itself and to turn one's energies to the cultivation of a mere reputation for justice—to merely *seeming* to be just—while also reaping those goods injustice can procure when properly disguised? Adeimantus in particular is quite concerned to show how the conventional praises of justice—not only those praises similar to Socrates' argument that communities require justice but even those grander praises in which the poets tell of great rewards given to the just in Hades as well as on Earth—deconstruct into the advice that one should merely pretend to be just. If a bright young man thinks through these praises, Adeimantus argues, he will discover that their true teaching is that one ought to draw "a shadow painting of virtue" around oneself while trailing behind this facade "the wily and cunning fox of the most wise Archilochus" (365c3–6; see especially 362e2–363e4 and 365a4–366b2).

The problem with defending justice in terms of other goods, however, runs deeper than this, or to put this slightly differently, the fact that the conventional praises of justice ultimately praise only the appearance of justice is just the first part of the problem that impels Glaucon and Adeimantus' insistence that Socrates defend justice in a wholly different way. The deeper problem can be seen by asking this question: What does it imply about justice itself that it is praised or defended in terms of other goods, that is, in terms of rewards? It implies, for one thing, that justice *needs* rewards. And there would seem to be two problems with this implication, or two further implications following from this one. First, to imply that justice needs rewards is to imply that justice is not attractive in its own right. (A large step is thus taken, precisely in the conventional praises of justice, down the road to the view that justice itself is not choiceworthy, that it is even *harmful* to the just man himself.) And second, to imply that justice needs rewards suggests that human beings are not capable of true justice: by bribing people to be just, to put it in the crude terms Glaucon and Adeimantus mean to capture, the conventional praises of justice seem to acknowledge that no one is ever just simply for the sake of justice itself, or out of true devotion to justice.

Now, with these two problems in view, we can turn more directly to the demand Glaucon and Adeimantus make of Socrates that he defend justice in and of itself, a demand that expresses a concern both with establishing the possibility of truly just action and with vindicating such action as the greatest good of the soul. Glaucon and Adeimantus go so far, in fact, as to demand that Socrates show that even in the midst of great suffering a truly just man will be able to stand by justice and that this will be good for him. That is, they want Socrates to show them that there can indeed be a truly just man—one whose justice will not bend even when "tested" (see 361c5–6)—and at the same time to prove that such a man's justice will make him happy despite the worst of circumstances. Glaucon poses the challenge more starkly than Adeimantus does, and from here on we may focus on his speech.[2] Imagine, Glaucon says, a man of such perfect injustice that he has all the ordinary goods of the world—not only goods like money and sexual pleasure but even such things as ruling offices and friends—and on the other hand imagine a man of perfect justice who, out of his devotion to true justice and not its mere appearance, is persecuted and tortured because the inner purity of his just soul is not manifest to others: Now show me that the just man is happier! This extraordinary challenge would seem merely crazy were it not understandable as the radicalization of two aspects of justice. First, Glaucon means to capture and isolate the sacrifice and devotion of true justice. Glaucon strips his perfectly just man of all other goods because only by proving capable of giving up everything else can the just man show that he is just for the sake of justice itself rather than for its rewards (see 361b8–c3). Glaucon makes this test so severe that he insists that, in order to prove his true justice, the just man must be able to endure persecution even to the point of death (361c5–d1). Again, only by testing the just man's justice against all ordinary goods, even against life itself, can Glaucon bring out the meaning

---

2. The concerns of Glaucon that I will try to bring out in what follows, as well as the tensions in what he requests of Socrates, are present in Adeimantus' speech as well (see especially 366d5–e9 and 367a5–c5). I mentioned above, however, the reasons for focusing on Glaucon's speech (see p. 123).

and test the possibility of pure justice, sought for its own sake and esteemed as a principle higher than any other concern. Yet, it is precisely such justice that Glaucon wants to be shown is the greatest good of the soul. If Glaucon attends, in other words, to justice's demand of sacrifice and devotion, he also is moved by the promise that justice can be one's own deepest or truest good.

There is a difficulty, to be sure, in Glaucon's request because of these two strands. The difficulty can be stated simply. If justice is truly a sacrifice, how can it also be one's own deepest good? Or, more importantly, if justice is truly one's own deepest good, does it really make sense in the end to think of it as a sacrifice? Precisely if justice is good, it would seem that it *cannot be* a genuine sacrifice. The difficulty can be put another way: Glaucon presses as hard as he can (see 361d7) the claim of justice to be a principle higher than the good, that is, to be more important than one's own good, and he is greatly concerned with the nobility of sacrifice on behalf of justice so understood; yet, at the same time, by asking to be shown that justice is the greatest good of the soul, he subordinates justice to the good. Indeed, lest we overlook the woods for the trees, this last point is the most obvious point in Glaucon's whole speech. Since Glaucon makes the choiceworthiness of justice contingent on its goodness, the good is the highest standard for Glaucon, not justice. Yet, in light of the fact that Glaucon contradicts himself by demanding that justice be a sacrifice and also be good, or in light of the problem that he affirms, even as he makes the case for justice as the highest consideration, that the good is truly his highest concern, we should wonder whether we have yet fully grasped why Glaucon makes such an extreme request, demanding that the just man give up everything else for the sake of justice. What does this extremism indicate?

To answer this question, it must be granted that the tension or contradiction in Glaucon's request is perhaps not as evident as I have just made it seem. In fact, the two points Glaucon insists on—namely that justice must at once involve great sacrifice and at the same time make the just man happy—are, in a crucial way, connected. We can understand this connection by thinking further about the character of the promise that justice holds out that it can be one's own deepest good. For doesn't this promise first come to sight as the promise that a life lived in devotion to something higher than oneself is a better and more satisfying life than one lived only for oneself? And isn't justice most beautiful, and thus this promise most intense, when one is asked to sacrifice all other goods—or even one's own life—for justice? While Glaucon worries that justice may not be true to its promise and worthy of his devotion (hence the necessity of his request to Socrates to show that it is), it is important to grasp that neither is he satisfied with the life of the unjust man that he describes in his speech (see 362b2–c6; also 360b6–c3, 360e6–361b5). And it may be not only the wickedness or selfishness of that life that troubles him but also his awareness that any happiness belonging to such a life would be fleeting and incomplete in a way the happiness found in the devotion to justice promises not to be. If so, Glaucon thus gives us a glimpse—even in the midst of expressing his fears that justice may not be worthy of his devotion—of the greatest hopes he attaches to justice. Indeed, to put the point more simply, Glaucon's fears, expressed through the vehement attack on justice that he reports to Socrates, would seem to be only the dark side of his hopes. The ultimately more important question, then, in trying to understand his speech, is not why he has come to have doubts about justice, but why his attachment to justice nevertheless persists. What are Glaucon's hopes, the hopes that sustain his belief in justice and may in turn be sustained by it? Following Glaucon's own lead, we may say that his hopes seem to be to find in justice the source of a truer happiness than that which belongs even to activities like ruling over cities, enjoying one's wealth, having sex with whomever one wants, and prevailing over one's enemies (see 362b2–c6). This is not to say that Glaucon fails to see the appeal of such goods; but he seems to be aware that that appeal is limited, as it must be given the transience and finitude of these goods. And Glaucon's deepest hope may be that such transience and finitude can somehow be overcome, or that justice can be a perfect good.[3]

---

3. Again, the just man whom Glaucon wants to see "tested" against the perfectly unjust man is one whose devotion to justice remains unwavering even "to the point of death" (361c3–d1). And it is this very man, who dies for the sake of justice, whose happiness Glaucon wishes to believe can surpass that of a man who enjoys every worldly good and satisfies his every desire (see 361d2–3).

On the general point regarding hopes attached to justice, compare Aristotle, *Nicomachean Ethics* 1129b25–29, taken together with 1097b14–16.

Justice as the Proper Order of the Soul

Still, whatever Glaucon's hopes may be, they do not remove—if anything, they deepen—the central difficulty in his speech, and his request to Socrates remains contradictory. This may be why Socrates responds to Glaucon and Adeimantus by first expressing his inability to respond: "I can't help out, for it seems to me that I'm incapable of it" (368b4–5; see also, between the two speeches, 362d7–9). To be sure, Socrates acknowledges that neither can he simply say nothing in response to Glaucon and Adeimantus: he fears, he says, that it would be impious not to give some response when justice has been attacked (368b7–c2). Socrates' full response, of course, takes the form of the rest of the *Republic*, with its many features and conundrums. But to return now to our earlier consideration, perhaps the most elevated strand of Socrates' response is his presentation of justice as the proper order of the soul. When Socrates and Glaucon finally arrive at this definition of justice near the end of Book Four, Socrates reflects back on their efforts to discover justice: "our dream has been brought to its perfect end," he says, for in justice in the city as each class performing its own task "we may have hit upon an origin and model of justice" (443b7–c2). Justice in the city, while only a phantom of justice itself (443c4–7), seems at the end of Book Four to have provided the model for true justice, which Socrates describes in a remarkable speech:

> In truth justice was, as it seems, something of this sort, yet not concerning the external business of an individual but concerning what truly bears on him and his own. [The truly just man] doesn't allow each part in him to mind the affairs of others or the classes in his soul to meddle with each other, but he really sets his own house in good order; he rules himself, orders himself, becomes his own friend, and brings the three parts into harmony, just like three notes on a harmonic scale—lowest, highest, and middle. And if there turn out to be some other parts in between, he binds all of them together and becomes completely one from many. Moderate and harmonized, this is how he acts—if he acts in some way—either concerning the acquisition of money, or the care of the body, or some political matter, or concerning

private contracts. In all of these actions, he believes and names a just and noble action one that preserves and helps to complete this state of soul, and wisdom the knowledge that governs this action; but an unjust action he believes and names one that destroys this state of soul, and ignorance, in turn, the opinion that governs this action. (443c9–444a2)

But can what Socrates describes in this speech—the concern of a man for his own soul, a concern that may not even involve others or any political action (*"if* he acts . . ."*)—really be called *justice?* And how does this portrait respond to the concerns that found their most powerful expression in Glaucon's speech?

Socrates' definition of justice surely departs from or transforms Glaucon's understanding of what justice consists in. Indeed, not only does the man devoted to setting his soul in order seem a very different man from the self-sacrificing hero of Glaucon's speech, but he also seems to bear little resemblance even to more moderate versions of what a just man is—for example, Polemarchus' helper of friends and harmer of enemies or Cephalus' scrupulous payer of debts. The question, then, is whether there is some way of connecting these more common understandings of justice with Socrates' paradoxical definition. What path might there be from the more familiar ground expressed by Glaucon, Polemarchus, and Cephalus to the stranger result suggested by Socrates?

Now, in the concluding reflection at the end of our study of Book One, I suggested that the impetus to redefine justice arises above all out of the concern for the goodness of justice. That concern, however, took many forms in Book One, beginning with the simple acknowledgment by Cephalus that an action with obvious and immediate harmful effects cannot be called just. Let me suggest here that what we gain by supplementing Book One with Glaucon's speech (in particular) is a more complete view of this concern in all of its complexity and in one of its most impressive forms. If Book One already showed us that the goodness of justice is complicated—for, as Thrasymachus was so eager to emphasize, justice is also a restraint on our pursuit of our own good—Glaucon gives us the best indication of how the very problematic character of justice's goodness is closely tied to the greatest promise raised by justice. The problematic character of justice's goodness is captured in a certain way in Glaucon's attempt to isolate justice as pure sacrifice and devotion. Yet, if Glaucon even goes so far as to suggest—by portraying justice as a sacrifice—that justice is *not* good, that it is even *harmful* to the just man himself, Glaucon also proves unwilling to leave matters at that, for he expresses also his hope to find in such sacrifice his own highest perfection. And isn't Glaucon here simply giving voice, in a particularly powerful way, to the ordinary understanding of virtue, at the heart of which lies both the demand for sacrifice and the claim to be our highest perfection and thus our deepest good? Although Polemarchus briefly expressed the thought before him (335c4–5), Glaucon gives us the fullest view of what is meant and hoped for in the thought that justice is virtue.

In the thought that justice is virtue, however, lies a concern that does not come fully to light in our pursuit of more ordinary goods. As Glaucon helps us to see, ordinary goods, while they are undeniably good in an obvious way, are just as undeniably good in a limited way. By promising not only to gratify us but also to perfect us, justice, by contrast, opens up a certain question that might otherwise remain closed: the question of the true good or the best life. The question of the best life, one could say, is the fully conscious response to justice's promise to be a good greater than the goods of ordinary life. Yet, to bring this back once again to the question of justice defined as the proper order of the soul, it may be that once the question of the best life comes into the open, we cannot rest satisfied with the most immediate answer that justice as it is ordinarily understood would seem to give to this question, the answer, namely, that the best life consists in devotion and sacrifice on behalf of justice. Or, to put this another way, it may be that justice has to undergo a transformation in meaning to sustain its claim to be our true perfection. The need for such a transformation can be seen not only in the kinds of difficulties Book One brought out in the ordinary understanding of justice, and not only in the confusion or incoherence of Glaucon's request, but also in another aspect of Glaucon's character or state of mind, an aspect that Socrates will suggest at the end of the *Republic* is characteristic of all who practice virtue without philosophy: as much as Glaucon loves justice, his love, as we have seen, is not free of doubts and reservations (compare 619b2–e5). By his own account, Glaucon is fully convinced neither that the unjust life is the best life *nor* that the just life is (see 358b1–d3). And Glaucon's speech, capturing as it does not only the beauty of justice but also its cost and the allure of injustice, is elegant testimony that Glaucon is not wholehearted in his love of justice, or that he is torn. Now, Glaucon's doubts and reservations are perhaps only to be expected given his understanding of virtue. But would true virtue divide us in this way? Or would it rather have the consistency and harmony we see in Socrates' picture of the well-ordered soul? From this point of view, is it not possible to see Socratic virtue—a virtue of self-perfection without self-overcoming—as a kind of transformation or "purification" of the ordinary understanding of virtue that is required to make virtue, as far as we can reasonably wish, the untainted good it seeks to be?[4]

To be sure, this transformation goes quite far in the *Republic*, for Socrates ultimately comes to equate justice with philosophy, a further movement that may be understood as the spelling out of what it means for the soul to be properly ordered with reason as its ruler. But if this movement travels far beyond the ordinary understanding of justice, the important point is that it is not without some basis in the ordinary understanding. For the ordinary understanding of justice gives us perhaps our first access to the question of the best life or what is good for the soul. And if the answer to this question ultimately proves to be the rule of reason in the soul, it makes at least some sense to regard such rule as the attainment of justice.

---

4. It might seem incorrect to suggest that the rule of reason over the lower parts of the soul does not involve self-overcoming. Yet self-restraint is not yet self-overcoming in the decisive sense. Cf. 441c9–444e6, bearing in mind also that the account of the soul on which this presentation is based (437b1–441c7) may be merely provisional (see 437a4–10 with what precedes).

Conclusion

The conclusion that the rule of reason in the soul, which comes to mean philosophy, is the truest practice of justice is one of the extraordinary conclusions of the *Republic* that I mentioned at the outset of this study. It is also a conclusion which shows how large is the gap that ultimately emerges between Plato and Kant, who remains a much more steadfast defender of the ordinary understanding of morality and of the ordinary moral life as the best life. I began this study of the beginning of the *Republic* by suggesting that Plato's analysis of justice could pose a challenge to Kant's view of morality; I also suggested that, when seen in its true form, Plato's analysis presents an approach to the question of justice that is not vulnerable to the "anti-foundationalist" criticism more recent thinkers like Rorty have leveled against Plato. In conclusion, let me say a few words about the light that our study of the *Republic*'s opening sections has cast on these issues. Rather than trying to encompass or revisit every twist and turn our study has considered, I will emphasize a few crucial moments, especially the difficulty we have just seen in Glaucon's speech and the early movement—beginning with the weapons example—of Socrates' discussion with Cephalus and Polemarchus. For these moments are particularly instructive in bringing out, in the first place, the importance of beginning from ordinary moral opinions as they are most immediately expressed and proceeding dialectically rather than in the abstract, "foundational" manner depicted by Rorty in his caricature of Plato. Furthermore, these moments indicate the difficulty or even the impossibility that such a dialectical analysis reveals in simply affirming and defending ordinary moral opinion as Kant does.

On the deepest level, there is a similarity between the contradiction in Glaucon's speech and the early movement of the discussion with Cephalus and Polemarchus. The same difficulty, if in different forms, can be seen in both instances. For justice, if we speak of it broadly, can be said to first present itself to us as a set of principles that we should be unwilling to compromise, and that call for our devotion and readiness to sacrifice ourselves for an end higher than ourselves. This is true of justice, in one way or another, at all times and in all places; as introspection about what we most deeply admire will show, this basic aspect of justice still moves and inspires us today—despite the many effects of modern liberalism—as it also moved and inspired the likes of Polemarchus and Glaucon. When Rorty, for instance, points to the great variety of historical understandings of morality, he overlooks a core similarity, a similarity that I think both Plato and Kant would insist is more fundamental and important than the undeniable variety in many respects. Yet, to return to the character of this ever-present core of justice or morality, our study has brought out and dwelt on the fact that justice not only seems to call for devotion to a set of principles more important than any individual's own good, but it also promises to be good for us. We have just considered this promise in the form that it is expressed in Glaucon's speech. But Socrates' earlier discussion with Cephalus and Polemarchus revealed the importance of the goodness of justice in a simpler but perhaps more decisive sense. Cephalus and Polemarchus, as we saw, showed a willingness to *transform the very meaning of justice* so as to preserve its goodness. Polemarchus in particular, a young man whose attachment to justice is the least ambiguous of any of the interlocutors we have studied, was unwilling to accept as justice—as something possessing the impressiveness and seriousness he expected of justice—something that was shown to be of defective goodness. His affirmation that justice is human virtue (335c4–5), when considered together with his other agreements (see again, e.g., 332a11–b4, 334d3–11, 335d7–9), can be seen as an affirmation that true justice must not only require devotion and sacrifice, but must also contribute to the just man's own fulfillment.

These results pose a problem for Kant's project of simply articulating and defending ordinary moral opinion and deferring to its judgments, especially its judgment regarding the primacy of duty. For ordinary moral opinion, to sum up the difficulty brought out by the opening sections of the *Republic*, is not fully consistent or coherent, and as much as it, or rather its representatives, seem to affirm the primacy of duty, they also affirm the importance of a point that calls this primacy into question. Now, it may be true that the ordinary understanding of morality can be made impregnable to critique by rigorously insisting upon that strand of it that demands unconditional devotion and by refusing to grant equal status to the other strand, that which stresses the goodness of justice and promises happiness. Kant does this in his defense of morality. But in doing so, is he really true to the full complexity of the perspective he wants to defend? Isn't Kant forced to impose a coherence on, and thus to distort, a view that lacks perfect coherence on its own? In particular, doesn't Kant have to insist upon the subordination of a concern which, even if its full weight is not immediately apparent, proves to be essential to our convictions about justice and our desire to be just? These are questions that speak to the very basis or grounds of Kant's moral project. For Kant himself claims that the complex arguments and rigorous principles that make up his moral philosophy have their basis in the moral judgments of our "ordinary reason." He insists that he is doing nothing more than clarifying, affirming, and defending the view that is already present in the moral understanding of the most common intelligence.[1] But can such a view simply be clarified, affirmed, and defended if it is not fully coherent and does not truly maintain what initially appears to be its first principle? Such are the doubts that I think the Platonic analysis of justice raises about Kant's moral project.

The Platonic alternative to the Kantian project is one we have seen, or have begun to see, through our study of the opening sections of the *Republic*. It is not, as it is so often portrayed, an effort to discover some "foundation" for justice apart from the world of ordinary opinion, or an effort to deduce the principles of justice from an independent and prior understanding of the good or of the best life. Nor is it an anti-philosophic denial that the search for anything beyond the principles proclaimed by one's particular community is possible. Rather, it is a Socratic examination that begins from our

---

1. See, for example, *Groundwork*, pp. 71–73, *Critique of Pure Reason* A807/B835, "On the Common Saying," pp. 70–72.

most basic convictions about justice and thinks through their premises and complexity. This examination culminates not only in a revised or transformed view of what justice is, but it also brings to light and has a bearing on the question of the best life. That it has these latter results is to be expected from the former, since our convictions about justice play such an important role in our convictions about what is good for us. To see clearly, however, the full character of the best life as Plato understood it and presented Socrates living it, would require that we go beyond this study of the beginning of the *Republic*. It would require a study of the entire *Republic* and indeed all of Plato's dialogues.

Bibliography

The Oxford Classical Texts editions of the various ancient works cited will not be individually listed in this bibliography.

Adam, James. *The Republic of Plato.* Edited with critical notes, commentary, and appendices. Volume I. Cambridge: Cambridge University Press, 1965.

Ahrensdorf, Peter J. *The Death of Socrates and the Life of Philosophy: An Interpretation of Plato's Phaedo.* Albany: State University of New York Press, 1995.

Alfarabi. "Plato's *Laws.*" Translated by Muhsin Mahdi. In *Medieval Political Philosophy.* Edited by Ralph Lerner and Muhsin Mahdi. Ithaca: Cornell University Press, 1972.

Allen, D. J. *Plato: Republic I.* Edited with an introduction, notes, and vocabulary. Bristol: Bristol Classical Press, 1993.

Annas, Julia. *The Morality of Happiness.* New York: Oxford University Press, 1993.

———. *An Introduction to Plato's Republic.* Oxford: Clarendon Press, 1981.

Anscombe, G. E. M. "Modern Moral Philosophy." *Philosophy* 33 (1958): 1–19.

Averroes. *Averroes on Plato's Republic.* Translated by Ralph Lerner. Ithaca: Cornell University Press, 1974.

Benardete, Seth. *Socrates' Second Sailing.* Chicago: University of Chicago Press, 1989.

Bloom, Allan. *Giants and Dwarfs: Essays 1960–1990.* New York: Simon and Schuster, 1990.

————. *The Republic of Plato.* Translated, with notes and an interpretive essay. New York: Basic Books, 1968.

Bolotin, David. "The Life of Philosophy and the Immortality of the Soul: An Introduction to Plato's *Phaedo.*" *Ancient Philosophy* 7 (1987): 39–56.

————. *Plato's Dialogue on Friendship.* Ithaca: Cornell University Press, 1979.

Collins, Susan. "The Ends of Action: The Moral Virtues in Aristotle's *Nicomachean Ethics.*" Unpublished Ph.D. dissertation, Boston College, 1994.

Craig, Leon. *The War Lover: A Study of Plato's Republic.* Toronto: University of Toronto Press, 1994.

Cross, R. C., and Woozely, A. D. *Plato's Republic: A Philosophical Commentary.* New York: St. Martin's Press, 1964.

Dobbs, Darrell. "Choosing Justice: Socrates' Model City and the Practice of Dialectic." *American Political Science Review* 88 (1994): 263–277.

————. "The Piety of Thought in Plato's *Republic*, Book 1." *American Political Science Review* 88 (1994): 668–683.

Friedländer, Paul. *Plato.* Volume 2. Translated by Hans Meyerhoff. Princeton: Princeton University Press, 1969.

Galston, William. *Liberal Purposes.* Cambridge: Cambridge University Press, 1991.

Hardgopoulus, Demetrius. "Thrasymachus and Legalism." *Phronesis* 18 (1973): 204–208.

Henderson, T. Y. "In Defense of Thrasymachus." *American Philosophical Quarterly* 7 (1970): 218–228.

Hourani, George. "Thrasymachus' Definition of Justice in Plato's *Republic.*" *Phronesis* 7 (1962): 110–120.

Howland, Jacob. *The Republic: The Odyssey of Philosophy.* New York: Twayne Publishers, 1993.

Hume, David. *Enquires Concerning Human Understanding and Concerning the Principles of Morals.* 3rd ed. Oxford: Clarendon Press, 1975.

Irwin, Terence. *Plato's Ethics.* New York: Oxford University Press, 1995.

————. *Plato's Moral Theory.* Oxford: Oxford University Press, 1977.

Jang, In Ha. "The Problematic Character of Socrates' Defense Justice in Plato's *Republic.*" *Interpretation* 24 (1996): pp. 85–107.

Kant, Immanuel. *Political Writings.* Translated by H. B. Nisbet, Edited by Hans Reiss. Cambridge: Cambridge University Press, 1991.

———. *Critique of Judgment.* Translated by Werner S. Pluhar. Indianapolis: Hackett Publishing Company, 1987.

———. *Critique of Pure Reason.* Translated by Norman Kemp Smith. New York: St. Martin's Press, 1965.

———. *Groundwork of the Metaphysic of Morals.* Translated by H. J. Paton. New York: Harper Torchbooks, 1964.

———. *Critique of Practical Reason.* Translated by Lewis White Beck. Indianapolis: The Bobbs-Merrill Company, 1956.

Kautz, Steven. *Liberalism and Community.* Ithaca: Cornell University Press, 1995.

Kerdford, G. B. "Thrasymachus and Justice: A Reply." *Phronesis* 9 (1964): 12–16.

———. "The Doctrine of Thrasymachus in Plato's *Republic.*" *The Durham University Journal* 9 (1947–1948): 19–27.

Klein, Jacob. *A Commentary on Plato's Meno.* Chapel Hill: University of North Carolina Press, 1965.

Lycos, Kimon. *Plato on Justice and Power: Reading Book I of Plato's Republic.* Albany: State University of New York Press, 1987.

Maguire, J. P. "Thrasymachus . . . or Plato?" *Phronesis* 16 (1971): 142–163.

Melzer, Arthur. *The Natural Goodness of Man: On the System of Rousseau's Thought.* Chicago: University of Chicago Press, 1990.

Nettleship, Richard Lewis. *Lectures on the Republic of Plato.* London: Macmillan and Company, 1925.

Nichols, Mary. *Socrates and the Political Community: An Ancient Debate.* Albany: State University of New York Press, 1987.

Nussbaum, Martha. "Non-Relative Virtues: An Aristotlean Approach." *Midwest Studies in Philosophy*, Volume 13, edited by Peter French, Theodore Uehling, Jr., and Howard Wettstein. South Bend: University of Notre Dame Press, 1988.

Pappas, Nickolas. *Plato and the Republic.* London: Routledge, 1995.

Rawls, John. *Political Liberalism*. New York: Columbia University Press, 1993.

———. "Justice as Fairness: Political not Metaphysical." *Philosophy and Public Affairs* 14 (1985): 223–251.

———. "Kantian Constructivism in Moral Theory: The Dewey Lectures." *Journal of Philosophy* 77 (1980): 515–572.

———. *A Theory of Justice*. Cambridge: Harvard University Press, 1971.

Reeve, C. D. C. *Philosopher-Kings: The Argument of Plato's Republic*. Princeton: Princeton University Press, 1988.

Rorty, Richard. *Objectivity, Relativism, and Truth*. New York: Cambridge University Press, 1991.

———. *Contingency, Irony, and Solidarity*. New York: Cambridge University Press, 1989.

Sachs, David. "A Fallacy in Plato's *Republic*." *Philosophical Review* 72 (1963): 141–158.

Salkever, Steven. "Virtue, Obligation, and Politics." *American Political Science Review* 68 (1974): 78–92.

Sallis, John. *Being and Logos: The Way of Platonic Dialogue*. New Jersey: Humanities Press International, 1986.

Sandel, Michael. *Liberalism and the Limits of Justice*. Cambridge: Cambridge University Press, 1982.

Schiller, Jerome. "Just Men and Just Acts in Plato's *Republic*." *Journal of the History of Philosophy* 6 (1968): 1–14.

Schleiermacher, Friedrich. *Introductions to the Dialogues of Plato*. Translated by William Dobson. New York: Arno Press, 1973.

Simpson, Peter. "Contemporary Virtue Ethics and Aristotle." *Review of Metaphysics* 45 (March 1992): 502–524.

Sparshott, F. E. "Socrates and Thrasymachus." *The Monist* 50 (1966): 421–459.

Stallbaum, Godofredus. *Platonis Opera Omnia*. Edited with an introduction and commentary. Edited by Leonardo Taran. New York: Garland Publishing, 1980.

Strauss, Leo. "The Origins of Political Science and the Problem of Socrates: Six Public Lectures." *Interpretation* 23 (1996): 127–207.

———. *The City and Man*. Chicago: University of Chicago Press, 1964.

————. *Natural Right and History.* Chicago: University of Chicago Press, 1953.

————. "On a New Interpretation of Plato's Political Philosophy." *Social Research* 13 (1946): 326–367.

Vlastos, Gregory. *Platonic Studies.* 2nd ed. Princeton: Princeton University Press, 1981.

Walzer, Michael. *Interpretation and Social Criticism.* Cambridge: Harvard University Press, 1987.

————. *Spheres of Justice.* New York: Basic Books, 1983.

Index

143